ETERNAL BAGGAGE

It's Always Apart of Us

A Memoir By

JANEE S. DOMINO

Copyright © 2021 Janee Domino

All rights reserved. No part of this book may be reproduced, stored, or transmitted by any means—whether auditory, graphic, mechanical, or electronic—without written permission of both publisher and author, except in the case of brief excerpts used in critical articles and reviews. Unauthorized reproduction of any part of this work is illegal and is punishable by law.

PREFACE

Have you ever looked in the mirror and thought, "How'd I get to this point in my life?" I often scrutinize, "How in the fuck did I make it to this point?" I mean no one has had a perfect life! Mine is far from being a Victorian home with a white picket fence. Unless you're thinking of tv shows like 7th Heaven, Family Matters, or the Cosby Show, a perfect life is close to being unrealistic. Let's be honest, in real life everything is not what it seems. For example, Bill Cosby is a well known television star and he faced criminal charges for drugging a bunch of women to have sex with them! My theory about my life is that all the pain, drama, drugs, and money surrounded me like a time capsule levitating me through life to this exact point. My eternal baggage I continued to lug around, weighed my shoulders down, and made it impossible for me to enjoy life's possibilities. Throughout life I would try to leave an article at a time in the place I obtained it. I could no longer carry this baggage around. A lot of it shaped and molded my personality in a positive and unique way. Most of the time it hindered me from growing into the productive person I was destined to be. Consumed in everything around me, it finally struck me I never took the time to focus on me. All my life I have lived for other people being bounced around from one place to another, making a great impact on their lives. Nonetheless the people who have come and gone in my life, never made a positive influence on me. Over time I transformed into this ray of optimism and learned to turn my awful experiences into positive attributes and later rose above what I was expected to become. You wouldn't know the pain I suffered, because I learned to laugh my way through physical hell. One would say I am the complete opposite of my surrounding imminent chaos. In no way shape or form did I want to live the life that made people loathe me and think I had the "perfect" life.

CHAPTER 1

Staring out the tiny window of the airplane my adolescent brain slowly began to process this scene with familiarity. Deja vu sank in as the stewardess announced we would be landing in San Diego momentarily and we should return to our seats to safely put on our seat belts. I was going to live with my dad's eldest sister Aunt Gee and her daughter Tia who recently enlisted in the Navy. My cousin Tia was following our family member.s footsteps who also served in the military. Tia even promised to take me on a Naval Fighter Ship once I got settled in and enrolled in the nearby middle school. Being that I was the only child, I wasn't at all excited about the two children who awaited my arrival to ruin my lone wolf status. I liked other kids but I preferred to do my own thing. I was used to being the only child and did not look forward to being part of a trio.

Turbulence shook the plane making me cringe in my seat and I looked to my chaperone for reassurance that I was in good hands. She winked her eyes and said it would be over soon and I would be with my family when we landed. I could hear the screeching of the wheels gripping the landing strip as the plane's speed decreased and came to a halt at the terminal. I gasped for air, relieved the plane was no longer in the air. Feeling butterflies about going to live with my distant family I hadn't seen in years.

Anxiety began to overwhelm me and I started to have many thoughts. Would this living situation be like all the others and overwhelm me with displaced awkwardness? Each time I moved to live with someone I always felt alone. Never feeling welcomed, I opposed the good intentions everyone continued to express to help my mother by taking me in to live with them. Like all the other situations my mom always found herself in between a rock and a hard place. The rock being an alcoholic beverage and the hard place was finding someone to house me while she "got herself together" for the twentieth time. She was what one would call a functional alcoholic. At the time I never knew what being a functional alcoholic meant. Over time I began to see that despite some of her extra curricular activities, my mother was different from most of the women I encountered. My mom was a smart woman who always kept a well paying job in accounting and could dress to kill. Yet once again, here I was being shipped against my will to complete strangers while I await my mother's return. She wasn't perfect but I loved her nonetheless. It didn't matter what situations I was in, I always found my way back to her. So why did she always want to get rid of me, thinking that that was the best option?

    Aunt Gee's jolly little body shook as she waved her hands back and forth to catch my attention as I exited the plane. Tia looked different than I remembered, she was tall and resembled a supermodel. She didn't look like a Navy officer. Her two children stood next to her, a girl and a small baby. The little girl was cute and she was accompanied by her little brother who wore glasses. I had never seen such a small child with glasses. He reminded me of an African American Benjamin Button. I laughed to myself when I glanced at his tiny body dressed in a GAP outfit. I hugged each of them smiling and introduced myself.

    We waited by the turn dial at the baggage claim to retrieve my suitcase. My old fashion tan suitcase with a huge leather buckle across the front seemed to always hold all of my belongings. The handle held several tags from other flights I'd taken in the past. No matter where or whatever age I traveled, I always had the same suitcase. Shit, it was the only one I traveled with. I wasn't even off the plane for ten minutes and I was already ready to return back to what I knew as home. I missed East Palo Alto. In this moment I was feeling like I'd rather be with people I knew, than to be here with family I didn't know. I mean I knew of them but I didn't really know who they were personally.

Yes, I know I may appear to be pathetic. I would rather be sleeping on a pallet, on the floor of a roach infested home, with a house full of people would give me more comfort. Why was I here? I started to get overwhelmed, I didn't want to be alone with people who barely knew me. I wanted my mom. I wanted to be at my old school, even if I did have to fight with my peers every other day. I had grown to love that small 2 ½ square mile city known to be the Murder Capital in California. I missed my freedom. I was practically raising myself when I lived there. My mom was always working and how could Nanny keep up with us if she was confined to the house. I wondered what everyone was doing? Were they waiting for Nanny's friend Nick to arrive with leftovers so they could eat like kings and queens? Was someone causing a scene in the house because they were drunk or high? Was Nanny pulling her chrome 38° out to threaten their life for disrespecting her house? Who knows? At this moment I would rather be there then here. Did I weirdly miss the drama? Despite the negativity, it was the only place that would ease my mind and that I had grown to be accustomed to.

CHAPTER 2

I begged and begged my dad to let me go live with my mom and it was finally happening! Given my mom's long track record of being irresponsible at times and making poor life choices, my dad was quite apprehensive about the situation. I can't blame him! Shit he was still angry about my mom shipping me off to live with his elder sister, when I could've gone to live with him. Living with him is where I ended up anyway. I'm sure coming to live with him after my travels to San Diego made him even more upset. Nonetheless, my dad eventually gave in once I acted like the world was ending. I even fueled the fire by turning off all communication with him. He had no choice, my one man pep rally weighed in on his decision. I could tell he was furious and his attitude showed as he weaved in and out of the traffic on Highway 880 heading towards the Dumbarton Bridge exit.

Only a couple of months had passed since we had moved to Hayward, California. I was displeased with the school I attended. Martin Luther King Middle school wasn't for me! I dressed like a nerd and was casted out because I didn't wear the latest fashions. I was not hip with Jordan tennis shoes or wore Guess, Levi, or Girbaud clothing. For christ sakes I was 12 and still wearing my hair in fucking ponytails! I wouldn't have wanted to be my friend either.

Everyday for four months I walked to school alone. I watched helplessly while other kids socialized with their friends. I had no friends. Was I dead and this was all a dream? I felt like a ghost. I was completely transparent at school and at home there was no difference. My little sister who was about 6 months old, entirely erased me out of my father's eyes. My father spent all his free time taking my sister back and forth to daycare catering to her every need. Meanwhile I walked to and from school like a runaway slave in a down south forest. I made it my mission to be where I could be noticed and my plan was to go live with my mom. I was sure she would even give me the attention I needed. My preteen age consumed me with thousands of questions. What do I do if I get my period? How do I pick a bra when my breasts get bigger? How do I make friends? Why do I feel more comfortable in boy looking clothes than girl clothes? Am I a freak because I have no friends? I needed her now more than ever. I was truly lost in a pool of questions I didn't have answers to!

***

I swayed back and forth in the back seat of his two door Hyundai as he made a left onto University Avenue, another left onto the first street, followed by another quick left, ending with a right onto the final street. He quickly pulled up to a brown and white house on Tulane Street. I hardly noticed as I stared at all the street signs named after colleges or universities. Purdue, Fordham, Xavier, Gonzaga, Hunter; way too many to keep track of. Before I knew it I was standing curbside with my raggedy tan leather suitcase in my hand, alongside my father's red race rocket.

Normally when people are departing family or friends they feel sad and have a smidget of separation anxiety. Not me! I was not kicking or screaming! I had been running away in my mind what seemed like forever. The ton of bricks I carried on my shoulders was lifted when my feet hit the pavement. I bent down peering into the tinted passenger side window to say my goodbyes and I was blinded from the reflection of the sunset. Stuttering I said in a small voice, "bye Dad, thanks for the ride. I will call you later." He held back a flood of tears and slowly pulled away from the curb. I'm guessing his tears were from knowing I was making the worst choice of my life of wanting to live in the "Murder Capital of America". I had no idea East Palo Alto currently had the largest murder rate in the northern hemisphere. I watched his car pick up speed and make a right turn onto Georgetown Street disappearing out of sight.

Was I being selfish? Honestly I felt like he deserved a break. Now he didn't have to worry about me and could focus on my baby sister. I wasn't in their way anymore. I know my father loves me. Yet recently it wasn't physically being expressed due to the new bundle of joy delivered from the stork. I know you're thinking storks aren't real and are part of fairytales. Well I was Cinderella and I was trapped in the attic and my baby sister was being treated like a miniature princess. In my mind, my father had gone off to be with my evil stepmother and their new child and was never returning.

My leg braced the heavy suitcase as it slapped against my leg when I walked up the long walkway to the front door. The bright colorful four o'clock flowers that trailed the walkway were closed but I could still smell them while I waited patiently for someone to answer the door. I peeked around at the yard and saw different trinkets, flower pots, and beautiful flowers around the yard. The smell of greens and hammocks filled my nose when I leaned closer to peer into the dark black screen door. I knocked again. I heard someone approaching the door as they grunted like they were having a hard time to walk to the door.

"Who is it, God dammit?", she yelled out of breath. It was Nanny and she didn't seem happy to be answering the door. If it wasn't important to Nanny, it was obsolete in her mind. She was on a constant cycle. Wake up, drink coffee, smoke weed, put people in their places, manage a household of ex cons and drug attics, and from time to time pull her chrome revolver out for anyone who opposed her. She would repeat the cycle over and over and acquired her platinum grey hair that draped down her back along the way. Despite her negative Ora she was a sweet old woman who lived a hard life surrounded by an assortment of imbeciles. I loved her because she was real and most of all consistent. With Nanny you knew what to expect and it was nothing less than reality with a cutting edge of honesty.

"It's me Nanny. Janee, Patsy' daughter." it was the only thing I could murmur. The iron screen door swung open and standing before me was a large woman in a colorful moo moo gown and a soiled apron. She glared at me pushing her glasses up on her nose.

"Oh my god, it's you! You have grown so much! Your mom isn't home from work yet, get inside and get settled. I have an extra room key. I'll unlock the door for you."

I followed her inside and things were as I remembered. The living room was dark by the thick curtains that covered the windows. Three tall vintage China cabinets took up the dining area accompanied by a huge dining room table covered with ashtrays filled with cigarette butts, stacks of mail, folded clothes, soda bottles and any other household items you could think of. Attached to the dining room was a large living room with three large couches and a fold out futon lounge chair. The air was filled with greens and ham hocks, cigarette smoke, and the stench of piled up clothes stacked in their own storage spots throughout the living room. Everyone had their own corner or section in the living room where they kept their bags, containers, or drawer containing their clothes and anything that belonged to them.

I trailed behind Nanny to the middle door in the hallway. I was relieved. I expected to set up camp in the living room where I had done once before when I visited. Her keys jingle as she retrieves them from her apron pocket, pulling out what looks like a key ring belonging to a janitor. She cursed under her breath as she sorted through them to find the one that belonged to my mother's room door. Unlocking the door she hugged me and stepped to the side and said, "your mother will be home shortly when she gets off work. She works at a temp agency on Willow road in Menlo Park. She catches the bus, so it may be a while."

I thanked her and sat down on my mother's bed glancing around at how neat it was, differing from the rest of the house. Perfume bottles were aligned on her dresser with hygiene products and a couple of framed pictures of me, my uncles, and of herself. I hadn't seen my mom in a few months and remembered she had an accident cutting her Achilles tendon with a plate she dropped. An argument gone bad led to a dropped plate and a piece of the plate ricochet off the floor cutting the back of her ankle. From my understanding she damn near bled out in the kitchen and wore a cast for several weeks. Now she was mobile and was wearing a walking boot. Classic mother story with a shitty ending.

Bored from sitting in the room I placed my suitcase in the closet out of sight afraid to clutter her room because it was so organized. The change in my pockets jingled, reminding me of the money I "borrowed" out of my sisters piggy bank. She was too little to miss it anyway. I could use some shillings so I wouldn't be entirely broke on my travels to live with my mother.

Checking the amount of money I had, the smell of copper lingered in the air from my sweaty palms. Heading toward Nanny's room door I eased up the short hallway to the opening. Waiting to get her attention I stood silently in the doorway. After a while our eyes finally met. Softly I said, "Nanny may I walk to the candy house?" She agreed and handed me a dollar to bring her back a Pepsi.

On the other side of the houses parallel to Tulane Street was a trail that led to the Dumbarton Bridge. Being so close to the bridge the body of water under it causes a horrible marshy smell. The sun shined brightly and the wind blew, sending chill bumps over my arms. I walked up to the Candy House and rang the doorbell. A candy house is a small version of a store that carries items including chips, sodas, icees, candy, nachos, hot links, and other small food items.

As the door opened I heard a familiar raspy voice and snickering of other kids inside the light pink house. I knew that voice! From what I could remember that particular voice was always coaxing me into unwanted trouble and bossing me around. How would I ever forget her voice? She was always saying things like Nae nae do this or that? Could I have some? Do you want to go here or there? Knowing we were usually confined to the front yard or the neighboring streets near the house where we resided.

Yes it was definitely Kesha! She was huskier than most girls our age and her body filled out since the last time I remembered visiting her. She was dressed in a colorful floral 2 piece outfit mostly likely from the Durant Center in Oakland. She also wore matching "toe buster" sandals, an inexpensive sandal for girls that came in various colors that anyone could afford. Kesha pushed past Ari, Destiny, and the other girls and came to hug me. "Nae Nae you came to live with your mom at Nanny's?" I shook my head "Yea" feeling embarrassed she was making a big deal of me coming to live with them.

All the girls stood in awe watching Kesha showing a softer side than she normally does. She had tons of friends yet she was bossy towards them. None of them had never seen her show such a happy side! They all began to giggle and she immediately snapped back into her tough personality and yelled, "What's so deng funny?" No one answered afraid of what would happen if she disagreed with their response. She snapped grabbing my arm heading towards the sidewalk saying, "Lets go cousin. Forget them anyway. They think they're all that because they are light skinned and have long hair."

I trailed alongside her as she talked endlessly about every event that came to mind since our last encounter. I listened but my mind drifted towards the snacks I didn't get a chance to buy. I was most afraid about not buying Nanny's Pepsi. I wasn't starting off so good with my irreversible decision to come and live here. We arrived at the house and without blinking I lied and said they were out of Pepsi handing her the money back.

I watched in amazement while we stood in the front yard. Kids began to swarm toward and around us welcoming me back, since last the summer. Everyone talked at once and it was hard to decipher their lingo because they all spoke differently than I did. They spoke in slang terms, and I felt intimidated because it wasn't proper english. I was accustomed to adequately pronouncing words despite my lisp. The maturity showed when conversing and I had a broad vocabulary for my age. I was taught to read all the time and it displayed my intelligence when I opened my mouth. So I stood silently watching them interact and learned as much as I could before I was rudely interrupted by a loud voice.

"Yall kids need to move down the street with all of dat! Make sure you stay off my grass, because I take care of my yard!" said Nanny. For such a large woman she moved in silence and with grace. Her moo moo flowed in the evening breeze as she glided towards us, waving her hands back and forth for them to go away. "Yo' mama's bus will be by Costano in a few minutes. Start walking so you could go meet her. Mark you go with her! I don't need anything happening to that child before her mama sees her."

Kesha and I started off down Tulane waving goodbye to the group. I rubbed my arms because I was cold. I was not used to walking around at dusk, my dad would never allow that. She started talking about the guys she likes and went out with. Personally, I thought 12 years old was too young to have a boyfriend, but I listened anyway. "I hated boys", is what I thought. None of them were as good as me in sports. My dislike for boys made it difficult to be friends with them, when they envied my athletic skills. Of course, like always Kesha enjoyed making me uncomfortable in her own weird love hate way and bombarded me asking, "Have you had a boyfriend or ever kissed a boy?" I shrugged my shoulders. Emptiness overcame me. Deep down inside I truly hated boys, but didn't know why? In my mind, it was my mission to be better than them at everything.

The thought repeated in my mind of how they disgusted me. I was completely lost in thought and before I knew it we were at the bus stop across from Costano Elementary School. The loud motor and screeching brakes caught my attention. I turned to face the 6A bus coming to a halt in front of us. A warm feeling came over me once I smelled my mother's perfume. I could smell her before she even exited the bus when the doors opened. "Mom!", I yelled as she grabbed me and hugged me tight, making me forget all about boys.

CHAPTER 3

Today began ok but ended in a way that was beyond normal. Kindergarten for me was a walk in the park. Most of the kids cried all day, and I had no clue why they were so upset. Everything was so easy. I learned most of the things they taught now in preschool. How much did one have to do to excel in daily carpet time, cutting and pasting, coloring, counting, and writing alphabets? My favorite time was nap time because I loved when it was quiet. Cuddling with my blanket was so relaxing and I often was in the group to fall asleep first. My nap was more preparation for my adult like afternoons that were to come.

Nonetheless, my cousin and I were only 5 and we're responsible for ourselves after school was dismissed. Everyday consisted of our walk, 5 long blocks with our older cousin to her house.

During the week without any fears we walked together and alone past the neighborhood park down Fordham, my home on Gonzaga St., the corner store market on Clark Street, and two more blocks to our destination on Runnymede Street.

The home we had at daycare was the biggest home on Runnymede Street. Our 2nd cousin had a lot of kids so it was perfect for her huge family. The white structure was two stories high with countless windows. I would often imagine it to be a huge castle. The spacious rooms made it fun to run around inside during our games of hide and seek. No one could ever find me, so sometimes I gave in just so I could be the seeker. Outdoors was a large backyard that had tall trees and even a small guest house. Our activities were limited to hide and seek, playing in the trees, watching He-man, and doing our weekly homework packet. Time always flew past and we would be home before we could even think about it.

Today, I was picked up by my uncle Andrew, my mom's baby brother. He was a teenager at the time and my caretaker when my mom wasnt present. My uncle was always stepping in to come get me from daycare, school, or doing anything to take care of me. Uncle Andrew was really quiet and not like most boys his age. He was respectful and didn't sell drugs like all the neighborhood boys. He was caring, nurturing, and made good decisions. He was special. Out of my mom's five brothers, he was definitely my favorite because he made sure I was always safe and taken care of.

We arrived home to our 3 bedroom home on Gonzaga Street. It was quite gloomy. Clouds formed in the sky as if it may rain soon. My uncle unlocked the door and allowed me to walk in first. "How was school Nae nae?", he said, breaking the silence. I simply thought to myself "it was boring" but I didn't answer out loud. "Suit yourself, I know you're not much of a talker.", he replied, disappearing out of sight. Before I could even put my backpack down he returned with a peanut butter and grape jelly sandwich. Yes! My favorite sandwich, "Thank you uncle. I love you!" I said finally, finding the courage to speak.

My words had finally found their way to the surface. I hadn't spoken much all day and didn't have the energy to. I sat thinking about what happened on our walk home today. Kesha and I were alone today as we walked to our daycare. Our elder cousin stayed home sick. We didn't know we were really, really walking home alone today. It became concrete when my cousin's 3rd grade teacher handed me work for her to complete this weekend. We were at ease to see there was a group of kids that walked in front of us. We played, talked and laughed on our walk, like any other day. That's when it happened!

The 3rd time the grey car passed us our suspicions of its existence made us alert. The driver didn't look frightening. He was middle aged with balding hair, thick bifocal glasses and no facial hair. Kind of reminded me of a weird looking elementary school teacher. Our suspicions of the car heightened and we began to get frightened by the grey car. It continued to drive past us repeatedly, only slowing down when he was next to my cousin and I or the other group in front of us. The creepy car took turns stopping by us and the other group asking us dumb questions like "did we want candy?" or "did we need a ride?" My cousin and I knew better, we don't talk to strangers! We didn't even answer him or looked in his direction. With our eyes staring straight, we ignored him and kept walking.

We proceeded up Fordham street once we passed the park, the group in front of us diminished down to one. The girl walked in front of us and each time the creepy man would stop, she was the only person who acknowledged his presence. The light grey sedan finally made an illegal U-turn in the middle of the street passing us on the opposite side of where we walked. He was now driving slowly behind us! Growing tired of him weirdly stopping by us, my cousin and I took off running full speed up the street. I looked back to see if we were a safe distance away and I saw his hand stretched out toward the passenger window with a candy bar. The car door slowly opened and the little girl disappeared behind the closing door of the light grey car. We ran as fast as we could and never looked back.

My cousin and I knew what happened, but we never spoke of that day. It was one of our many secrets we kept tucked away hidden from anyone to know. I often thought if the girl was ok or if someone ever found her? The school never talked to us about it and I don't remember seeing anything on the news. My young age kept me distant from reality and it's harmful truths. We kept quiet as we walked the last couple of blocks to daycare cautiously scanning for the creepy grey car. Safely we made it to the white fortress on Runnymede Street. We closed the heavy door distancing the previous situation far behind us.

**

My mom returned home from "work" after the sun had already set, so I doubt if she had came straight home. It was Friday and that explains why my uncle picked me up from daycare today. I could hear her and her loud ass friends in the living room. Children were taught to speak only when spoken to and to stay in a child's place! I knew better than to come out my room so I waited in my room trying to decipher the conversations that took place behind my closed room door. I could tell they had been drinking from their slurred voices and probably would be up all night too.

I just wanted to be alone with her for once. I enjoyed laying in bed with her watching Star Trek or the Andy Griffith Show and eating snacks. We usually did that on Saturdays and Sundays. She would party so much that she would be too tired to get out of bed. So I took advantage of those times to relax and spend time with her when I could.

There were times I didn't want to be left behind, so I would sneak and hide in the back seat of her two door Monte Carlo. She would be too intoxicated to notice I was there. I would hear her talking shit to other drivers and hold on tight as she raced through the dark streets to the local liquor stores. There were times when she would pull up to the drug dealers and buy dope too! I know my mom loved alcohol and she would talk about how alcoholics ran in her family. Never knew her to like or use drugs. I think she just bought it so she could give it to her friends and to seem cool to hang out with. Maybe I was naive to the fact she was a closet smoker.

I fought the urge to stay in my room and finally got the nerve to come out when I heard my mom say she was leaving. I just wanted to be with her. She hugged me tight when she saw me and smelled of perfume, alcohol, and cigarettes. I didn't care. I still hugged her back tightly, almost not letting go. "Ok Nae Nae, I'm leaving now." She said.

"I wanna go mom, please!", I pleaded.

"No baby, you can go next time, I promise."

"You always say I can go next time mom. I wanna go with you now. Please?"

After pleading with her she finally agreed to let me go. I snuggled up in the back seat as the night air hit my chest. We didn't travel far and were at our destination before I knew it.

Looking around as I got out the car I could tell we were in Fordham. I remembered walking past this house before but never really paid too much attention to it. All the homes in the Village neighborhood were all built with the same design so you knew what to expect when you entered any home in this area. When we walked in it was dark and I was given a cover and directed to a musty old couch on one side of the living room. I tried to make out the various shadows as I watched my mom disappear into the hallway with her male friend.

My arm grew tired as I rested my head on my hand, trying to fight my sleep. Two young boys had weaseled their way into the dimly lit living room, playing around to gain my attention. They were older than me. They looked like two small, ugly, old men running around acting foolishly. My face showed how irritated I was and they eventually stopped goofing around and got quiet enough for me to drift off to sleep.

I tossed and turned as I dreamed people were touching me and pulling at my clothes. I dreamt that I was running and they grew closer and closer entrapping me. I couldn't see who was chasing me but I called out to my mom for help but she didn't help me. This nightmare began to feel all too real when I awoke and one of the boys was under my cover. Disgusted at what I saw I felt his hand come from my pants and he quickly jumped up and ran disappearing into the dark hallway. Why was his hands in my pants? That wasn't right, no one should be touching me down there! I sat up quickly and I noticed my pants were undone. I buttoned my pants and called out for my mom. She didn't answer. The quiet conversations that once took place in the darkened hallway were now silent. The house was completely dark and only the moonlight showed through the cracks of the curtains in the living room.

I didn't feel right. I felt yucky and gross. It was my fault his hand was in my pants. I shouldn't have gone to sleep. Or maybe I shouldn't have begged my mom to come. I should have stayed home. Lord please make it go away! Why did this happen to me? My mom will be so mad at me if she finds out. I hate boys because boys do mean things. I wanted to kill him whatever his name was. When I get older and stronger I'm going to kill him and make him feel pain, like I feel right now.

I watched the sun rise and the light trickled into the living room revealing it's old fashioned decorum. I hated this place. I waited anxiously for my mother to awake and it seemed like forever. Fed up with waiting I quietly snuck out the front door and started to walk home. My eyes scanned the streets looking for stray dogs that were known to be out at this time of the morning. I hated walking in the morning but I didn't want to be there at that mean old house. I finally turned the corner onto Gonzaga Street and could see my home. My uncle stood in the yard and waved when he saw me. My head hung low as I stared at my feet when I passed him heading to the front door. He shook his head and said he loved me as I closed the door when I entered the house.

My mom cursed at me. Her raspy voice seemed far away as she yelled at me for leaving the house we were at, without asking. I didn't reply as I stared at her wishing I was somewhere else. She offered for me to join her and watch tv but I declined. I stayed in my room all day that day, thinking how much I hated myself and most of all how much I hated?

CHAPTER 4

I don't remember how or when we began living with our cousin Scarlet, at the party house. Kindergarten had ended, the weather was always hot, and the school year ended briefly before our move. It was the summer of 1984. We eventually lost our home on Gonzaga Street and were now living with another cousin of ours on Illinois Street. Company was always over and playing loud music was the norm. I was unaware I was living in the middle of a Crack infested home! It became apparent after I watched the steady foot traffic, especially during the evening. The silent hand to hand exchanges of nothing made me realize the hand is definitely quicker than the eye. I never saw money or drugs exchanged but I knew something was being exchanged for something!

Sometimes I was sent to stay the night with Scarlet's daughter Olivia. Olivia was about 18 or 19 years old with a lot of children and she lived in her own home on Notre Dame Street. I would often spend the night, so one extra child didn't make a difference. The children were much younger than I with runny noses and always had shitty diapers. They were the typical stereotype of black children. I hated being there! All they ate was noodles and Vienna sausages in the can. Their rooms always reeked of urine and dirty clothes. There was never anything to do. All their toys were either missing pieces or broken. There's no fun in that! Visiting her house was a complete disaster and failure to me living a promising childhood.

One memory in particular I will never forget impacted me to remember you always have to defend yourself no matter the circumstances. One day my cousin Kesha and I were playing in the backyard. My uncle accompanied us to make sure one of the vicious dogs that roamed around in the yard didn't attack us. We played in the water playfully, occasionally wetting each other.

Along came the mean BettyJean! BettyJean was the same age as my cousin and I, yet her olgarish body made her seem like a giant! Although she was our cousin she treated me like a can on the street and decided to kick me down figuratively whenever she felt like it. She was always picking on me and I always cried instead of fighting back.

My uncle grew tired of me always being a punk so to speak. I didn't know what a punk was! I just knew the way she acted towards me was mean. My uncle vowed to make me tougher and pulled me to the side to have a pep talk with me. Unaware of what awaited me, he filled me in that today was the day I would be fighting back. I watched him clear a space in the junk ridden backyard so we had a clear fighting area. My heart felt heavy and there was no way I could escape the fate that was decided without my consent. My palms were sweaty, everything around me seemed to move in slow motion and the sounds were distant. I wasn't ready, I was no match for her! My past encounters proved I wasn't adequate to fight her fair and square!

Both of us were brought to the center of the cleared dirt area and he said we were going to fight. Oh no, I was only six years old, I didn't know how to fight. All I knew how to do was cry and I was especially great at crying. I shook with fear when she approached me with her balled up fist.

One strike to my face and I fell to the ground bawling my eyes out. I stayed on the ground as she hovered over me daring me to get up. Sweat and dirt got in my eyes as I sat on the ground in fear of rising to my feet. My uncle snatched me up and pulled me to the side again. He dried my face with his t-shirt and told me to stop crying. In my mind I was done. There was no way I had any fight left in me. I lost before I even began. "Let this end now.", I repeated in my mind.

My uncle had other plans for me. I knew he did when I saw the tiny square canister hidden inside his ashy teenage hand. My vision was blurred from the bright sun and dust circling in the air like miniature tornadoes. I didn't know what he was pouring into my hand until I focused on the small pile in my sweaty palm. Pepper? How was tiny grains of seasoning going to make me not afraid or even a better fighter? Was I to eat it and grow angry from how spicy it was and turn into the Incredible Hulk? He whispered in my ear, "wait until she gets close to you Naenae and throw it into her face. Then beat her ass!" "That was the plan?", I thought. No way was that going to work. It's only going to make her even madder and then my beating will be even worse. I had nothing to lose, so pepper in the face it is!

"Round two!", he yelled. She came at me like a raging bull, and my fight or flight was activated for the very first time in my life. The confidence gleamed in her eyes showing this round would be easy because the first round proved her to be the better competitor. Without hesitation I stepped forward and lunged the pepper into her round sweaty face! A loud screeching cry howled through the backyard and throughout the neighborhood as she dropped to her knees. I did it, I actually did what my uncle said to do!

Wailing like a small puppy who had been stepped on by a large boot, she continued to cry out for her mother. At first I wanted to run when she hit the ground. There was no turning back now when I heard the cheers of my uncle Andrew and cousin Kesha to "get her". I began slowly punching her curly head as she lay helpless on the ground. Rage began to fill my body and before I knew it my punches increased thinking about all the mean things she had done to me.

My uncle snatched me off of her and drugged my aggressive body away from her. My cousin smiled at me giving me the look of approval that I had done what I was supposed to do. I felt respected. I knew what I had done was wrong but I felt relieved that I had made her feel what I felt every time she picked on me. No longer was I going to be bullied or feel uncomfortable when I was in her presence. Victory was bliss and it felt damn good to take control of my fate.

CHAPTER 5

Fighting was never one of my strong personality traits. I was always known to be a pushover or easily persuaded to do something. My cousin Kesha took advantage of that when she wanted something. Nanny was always asking me to make my famous smothered potatoes or getting me to clean up for her. My mother took advantage of the fact that I was a great kid, and thought I was mature enough to raise myself. She felt her presence was never needed, when having her around more was really important to me. Allowing people to manipulate my thought process and to help me into cheating my self worth became a pattern. I never decided or made decisions independently. Pitiful was my middle name.

Jack Farrell Park was the greatest place on earth if you were a tween or teenager who stayed in the Village Neighborhood. There was always some type of event like Children's Day, Juneteenth, baseball games, picnics, rugby, or basketball games going on. Despite its worn down look, "The Park " acted as a major social pastime for the good and the bad.

Mostly all the young children played tee ball or baseball and played at the park. The majority of the mothers of the children who played at the park were in attendance dressed to kill in their best outfits and best braided hair styles, looking to catch a new boyfriend or a new baby daddy. The women gathered and huddled in small groups eyeing the young females dressed in skimpy clothes that didn't have kids, but hung out anyway. They all talked loudly, swearing, smoking their cigarettes and blunts daring anyone to step to them so they could show their audience how tough they were. It wasn't a day that went by that all the baller drug dealers hung out in their fancy painted cars, sold drugs, and shot dice any and everywhere at the park. No matter what event took place their attendance was prompt and accountable. There was always an occasional fight to liven up the festivities. If you had a beef aka altercation with someone, the meet up to fight place was "The Park"!

I was new to the park and hadn't hung out there, not as a teen anyway. There was a lot going on and I felt lost trying to keep up with everything happening at once. I watched many children play on the rundown playground structure, throwing sand, and running wildly playing tag. Car engines roared as their drivers drove down the street quickly oblivious to the stop sign that stood in the middle of the block. The different candy painted cars looked like rainbows going back and forth displaying their rims and loud playing stereo systems. There was a dice game on the rear side of the building where the restroom was. The strong smell of urine lingered in the air whenever you walked past or was near the restroom. Guys shouted and laughed as they won or lost at every roll of the dice. Holding money in their hands, they squatted on their knees watching the dice roll up against the wall as if they were in Reno or Las Vegas.

My first teenage fight happened at the park. I wasn't prepared for what was in store for me. I had just moved back from living with my dad and everyone had met at the park to chill and hangout. A group of kids gathered around a few boys our age that had been recently adopted into the dope game. They showed off their money pulling it out of their pockets and caught the attention of girls willing to be their girlfriends.

One guy in particular named Dirty Ricky flexed his power by talking loudly and showing off his new Nike Tennis shoes. All the boys watched as he threatened the girls to wet them with his new toy, a "water weenie". He wasn't a bad looking guy. Take away the money and new shoes and it was clear to see why his name was Dirty Ricky. His good grade of hair was frizzy and in need of rebraiding but hung over his shoulders. The Guess Jeans he wore were filthy with dirt, and camouflaged in the stone wash pattern of the material. I cringed at his white tee that needed to be changed because it was covered with stains. Ugh, I couldn't see why everyone crowded around him. From what I saw his hygiene needed improvement, he was mean, rude, and by far a complete show off.

I thought to myself, "Please Lord don't let him bother me!" My prayers weren't good enough to keep him away. The distance I kept between us by standing at the top of the play structure never made a difference either. I watched him out of my peripheral vision to avoid any direct eye contact. His predatory instincts were like how a vulture can smell a dying animal. Ricky sniffed me out before I knew it. I panicked as I watched Ricky wet any and every child in his path. Just as I suspected he finally made his way to the top of the play structure. I froze in my steps afraid to walk past him. Fear eventually moved my feet. I tried to sneak by, while his attention was on another victim. I was too slow, he quickly squirted me in my face. Without thinking of the consequences I snatched the water weenie out of his hand. Everyone who witnessed it gasped, watching as he stood in shock holding only part of the toy in his hand. Not good! Anger filled his eyes as all the children broke out in laughter when they saw his water weenie was broken. I believe he thought they were laughing because I stood up to him. At this point none of the reasons mattered because he was furious! He glared around at them all laughing and snickering. In rage he landed a hard fist into the center of my stomach.

I closed my eyes, grabbing my tightened stomach as the pain grew inside my belly. I felt embarrassed and sick at the same time. My cousin Kesha could feel I was going to follow my first dumb move of breaking his toy with another dumb move of showing weakness and crying after he punched me. In a blink of an eye she stood between us yelling, "Leave my cousin alone with your dirty ass!" She held me up from falling as we headed up the tiny mound of dirt to the sidewalk. She swore and cursed at him until he turned red and threatened to beat her up too. She dared him, knowing he wouldn't take action.

I was relieved she saved me in a blink of an eye, or I would have been closed curtains! No one ever gave Kesha a hard time! She was like an evil villain to everyone with unbeatable super powers. Yet soft enough to always rescue me and be my hero! I held my stomach wishing I could disappear on the long walk home. "I hate boys, I hate boys, I hate boys", was on repeat in my mind. My cousin patted my back and said, "don't worry he'll never bother you again." At the time I really believed what she said was too good to be true. But she was right, he never did!

***

My cousin wasn't necessarily liked around the neighborhood but she was respected. Her loud mouth and blunt opinions of people relentlessly rubbed them the wrong way. I always found what she had to say enlightening and humorous. I was consistently guilty by association from laughter. I never cared when I heard gossip or quiet whispers involving her name. I was always safe when I was with her so I didn't care much about anything people had to say about her. I didn't care if people said she was ugly, mean, or their favorite word a "bitch". She was my protector and always came to my rescue. Wrong or right I was riding with her against the world.

Confusion often clouded my judgement of whether she was protective of me or if she only wanted me to be friends with only her. There were times when she picked arguments or lightly bullied people to push them away if she thought I was being friendly with them or vice versa. Countless times she has rescued me from the hyenas and vultures of the neighborhood. So I know she always meant well when it came to our friendship. Yet, her communication skills were lacking commitment of displaying true feelings. She hid behind sassy, witty comments, mixed with an array of curse words she had become accustomed to using profoundly.

Kesha's aggressive behavior had yet to be matched, even at her young age. Nanny described her as a "force to be reckoned with". Her presence was strong and could not be ignored wherever and whomever she was around. There was only one time I could ever recall her being frightened.

One evening on our way home from the park we were approached by a group of older boys. My cousin was well in doubt in certain body areas so she attracted older boys at times. The tall boys approached us continuously and asked her rude questions about sex. Scrunching our faces we tried to walk faster to avoid them and their inappropriate advances. I recognized two of the boys in particular when they continued to follow us yelling "Ay, ay, ay! Can we walk with yall?

Where's y'all boyfriends at?"

We continued walking but they caught up with us when we turned from Hunter Street onto Georgetown Street. I hated this street. In the neighborhood it was the absolute darkest of them all. The street lights were scarce and spread out and the huge trees made tons of dark shadows hiding any light that tried to shine through them. Dogs barked loudly at the sound of the boys yelling for our attention.

As they got closer Kesha took off running with me trailing behind her. Ducking into a nearby yard to hide we breathed heavily trying to catch our breaths. My chest burned because I forgot to wear a coat and the night bay air filled my lungs and squeezed them tightly with every breath. I could see them faintly through my watery eyes. We were separated as I continued to kneel down and go along the side of a parked car as they walked past the yard we hid in. Distracted from the chase she didn't follow my lead and follow along.

"Here she is!", yelled one of the boys. The other guy walked up behind him and they stood in front of her blocking her so she couldn't walk away from them. "Where are you going? You know you like us!", they said. She just kept saying, "Leaving me alone, don't nobody like yall!" in her raspy voice. They kept attempting to reach out and touch her like two octopus with 16 tentacles. She blocked every attempt, swatting their hands away yelling "stop!".

Her loud rebuttals trying to warn them away caught the attention of a nearby homeowner. Suddenly, a porch light came on, shining light on the uncomfortable situation of their mischievous and aggressive behavior . The porch light interrupted their attempts to be grabby with her, long enough for Keisha to break free. She ran up the street faster than I had ever seen her move in the past. I trailed behind her, even though I felt I was running at top speed. I was usually quite faster than her during sports or PE at school and I didn't catch up with her until she stopped running once we got to Tulane street. Glaring at me she said, "I thought you left me!" Shaking my head "no" her scared look turned into a smile. "I beat you running!", she said laughing. "You don't have wheels no mo'." "I hate them dumb ass niggas," She continued, shaking her head. "Me too", I replied out of breath.

"Awe damn the porch light is on! We are in trouble now!", Kesha said quietly. We turned the doorknob to the screen slowly to avoid it from squeaking. We crept into the living room sliding our backs against the curtains bumping our knees against the side of the couch. We did our best trying to avoid walking around the side of the couch facing Nanny's room. Nanny was quite clever in her technique of how she positioned mirrors in her room and in the living room to extend her view from sitting on her bed. We sat down flopping onto the couch relieved we had made it in unnoticed. Giggling to ourselves we heard a loud yell come from Nanny's room, "Get yo' fast ass in here now!" Our giggles and smiles turned to frowns as Kesha rose from the couch and walked in Nanny's room with her head down. Our attempts to come in unnoticed were ruined as she dragged her feet into danger, more than our previous encounter with the creepy boys before entering the house. Busted!

I could hear her trying to explain why we were late coming in. It was no use. Kesha's reasons of our tardiness were drowned in the yelling as Nanny's overpowering voice took the floor. She crushed Kiesha with tons of insults and assumptions of why we were late. I sat on the couch helplessly wanting to intervene and be the voice of reasoning but it wouldn't help. Nanny had made her decision a long time ago that her authority persevered any and everyone's opinion or thoughts. She was nonetheless the top dog in her household as she stated several times. What she said goes, and frankly there was nothing anyone could ever do about it.

Over time I learned there were two kinds of people Kesha feared, the creepy boys and Nanny the big bad wolf. I found no pleasure in knowing the one person I thought was fearless was submissive to an elderly woman and horny teenagers.

CHAPTER 6

My backpack weighs a ton with all the junk stuffed inside. The daily contents of my backpack consisted of my books, school clothes, shoes, and jacket. Toting around so many things made it hard to close, when I tried to zipped it up. I liked my hands free so I could bounce my basketball on my walk from the Rec Center. I loved going to the Rec. Any and everyone who played basketball went there in the afternoons to play. The Rec was my sanctuary and I loved going there after school. When I was there, I felt like a boss. My friend Donna and I were the most ruthless, female, 10th Graders ever to dominate the game of 2 on 2 Basketball amongst all men! Yes we were the Shit!

The tournament we played in today ended quickly for our duo. We lost in the 3rd round and were eliminated. No one likes losing and I was not great with taking a loss. I guess we did ok playing with cheating ass grown men. Not only were we females but we were also heightly challenged.

The thought never occurred to me how good I was back then. I should have been more grateful. Instead, I sulked in my self pity dragging my feet on my way home. I had hoped my stop at the store would cheer me up. I was like any other normal kid. Treating myself to my favorite snacks was definitely a luxury. I thought about what snacks to buy on my walk. Mystic or Snapple?

Reese's Peanut Butter Cup or M&M's? Hot fries or Sour Cream and Onion Lays?

I was beyond thirsty! I hated how dusty and rocky the streets were in the Midtown neighborhood. I truly believed the dust and the endless potholes were partly the reason I was always thirsty on my walks home. Inhaling all the dirt and particles that rose from the ground with every step and passing car filled my lungs and mouth increased my thirst for a cold beverage. The sun was literally melting me and made my eyes squint tightly as I walked up Bay Road. Cars traveled up and down Bay Road as if they were on the 101 Highway. Bay Road was adjacent to the 101 freeway which was on the other side of the brick wall parallel to the road. I bypassed the first store called One Stop, and the second store Oakwood Market. Finally stopping at Shop & Go I rushed into the store to feel the breeze coming from the loud fans positioned around the store. The breeze didn't compare to a functional AC but was more of a circulation of warm air that felt cool upon anyone's sweaty face who entered the bodega like market. The sun was setting and it was almost dark. I felt more comfortable shopping here because it was close to Ralmar Street and my house was two short blocks east of the corner store. I grabbed a Kiwi Strawberry Snapple, a bag of Nacho Cheese Doritos, and paid the store clerk.

The sound of the popping top when I opened my Snapple made my mouth water. It's cold fruity taste made me feel refreshed after drinking half of the bottle by accident. I put the top onto the bottle as I contemplated stuffing my snacks into my already full backpack. Lost in thought, I started to walk out the store and bumped into a tall stocky body. Almost dropping my basketball and my bag I looked angrily at the guy I bumped into. "Excuse you", I thought to myself, regaining my composure. I walked past him and suddenly I felt someone grab my arm.

"Nae Nae?", said the deep voice. "I knew it was you!" looking confused I clearly didn't recognize who he was. "It's me Dee, April's son!"

His persuasive tone to describe himself still didn't ring a bell or make me remember. I was still irritated from almost dropping my stuff and being stopped in my tracks. I shrugged my shoulders at his failed attempt to make me remember his existence. I was more focused on getting home. I ignored his callouts and kept walking trying to beat the setting sun.

I turned the corner of Bay Road onto Ralmar Street, briefly looking back trying to remember who the guy was. He knew who I was, which didn't surprise me. Tons of people know me and I have no clue who half of them are, when they speak to me. There was something very familiar about him and I could not place my finger on it. Only my family and people who knew me called me Nae Nae. If you weren't friends or family it just sounded weird calling me Nae Nae instead of Janee. His face was familiar and definitely the voice, but it wasn't ringing a bell in mind from where. My mind began to feel at ease when I could see my house. I always felt a sense of relief, once I reached the oddly placed Oak tree weirdly growing out of the middle of the street. Today I only felt my body get weak. I was tired from carrying my backpack, this bag, playing basketball, and walking all the way home.

The white metal screen door slammed behind me when I walked into the front door. Damn, that's all I needed to hear was my mother's husband complaining about slamming the door to "his" house. Luckily, he was engaged to the evening news, so he didn't even notice when I walked in.

Like clockwork my stepfather sat on the couch, basking in cigarette smoke, drinking his bottle of Jack Daniels Whiskey. I felt proud and relieved that my stealth-like arrival gave me an additional boost of energy to move quickly towards the hallway. He was vaguely aware of my presence; he spoke to me and I glided past him, high stepping down the short yet long hallway to my room. I peeked out the small window next to my room door before entering, searching for my little brother. He was always in the backyard with one of his friends, or building something with materials he took from his dad without permission. He was very crafty and could fix just about anything. I loved my little brother like he was my own flesh and blood. I could always count on him to be excited about basketball or music like I was. We had a lot in common. We loved sports, playing video games, and bike riding. I can honestly say, he was one of my favorite people in the whole wide world. When I looked out the window, he was nowhere in sight. I was too tired to go out back and look for him. I knew he would reappear soon, eager to persuade me to get into mischief.

Before flopping on my twin size bed, I opened my closet and tossed my backpack inside. Slowly I kicked my shoes off one by one reflecting on what happened at the store earlier. Who was that guy I thought hard to myself? As I pondered on where I possibly knew him from, bells rang in my head! Hitting me like a ton of bricks, it dawned on me who he was! He said his name was Dee but I remember him as De'Erick, my mom's ex-boyfriend little brother. Why didn't I remember him at first? Irritated on why I mentally blocked out his existence I gathered my belongings to go take a shower.

After showering I wiped the steam ridden mirror to reveal my reflection. I stared at my reflection thinking, "I'm hideous and definitely not that attractive". I rubbed my bare belly looking at how flat it was. Instantly I got disgusted with how big my chest and butt were and started to get dressed. I hated how boys made rude comments about my "big butt" or how I had a nice shape. Fucking gross! I did not want to be gawked at or be stared at in a creepy way as most boys did to me anyway. That was the reason I chose to wear baggy and boyish style clothing. In my mind the baggy clothes acted as a shield to hide what attracted the creeps. It never worked. They still were attracted to me like flies on shit. Most of the boys at school and at the Rec were the same. In my defense they all began upfront to want me sexually. The rest of them pretended to be my friend and ended up trying to get close to me to be more than friends. Most females my age would take their behavior as a compliment but I was repulsed by their actions.

I proceeded out the bathroom door and sat my stuff on the kitchen table. I quickly made my dinner plate trying to avoid having a conversation with my step father. He was ok, I guess. Today I just wasn't interested in his routine discussions about the oppression of the "black man", the idiots he dealt with today, or anything he's momentarily irritated with. He was a ball of too much negativity. Most of the topics he chose to discuss were usually after a bottle or two of Jack Daniels. Besides my opinions of him, he was a damn good cook, so he was temporarily ok in my book.

I scarfed down the food and my snack I purchased at the store. Rummaging through my backpack I found my binder to check that I did all my homework assignments. I usually did my homework at school. The work was so easy. I always finish my classwork and homework before the class period ends. For me there was plenty of time when I was done, to get in trouble for talking to my peers who weren't done working too. I turned on the TV and watched Dawson's Creek. I loved watching tv. Everything was always perfect or perfectly chaotic with a good ending. Why couldn't my life be the same as television sitcoms? Yeah right! Now I was asking for too much. Wanting my life to be like television was definitely wishful thinking.

My thoughts were interrupted when I heard my mom enter the house and the screen door slammed. She pushed my room door open, sat on my bed, and kissed me on my forehead. We talked for a little while. I told her about my day and about the basketball tournament.

Deliberately skipping small details about my day, leaving out running into Dee at the store. She exclaimed she was tired from driving in all the traffic and the long day she had at Intel. I totally understood that doing payroll for a multimillion dollar company could be tiring. She processed payroll for the Silicon Valley and Oregon branches. My mom worked hard and I didnt want to add to her stress by enlightening her of a memory I tried my best to suppress until now. She had to deal with my stepfather in his drunken state, which I am sure brought up feelings of her alcoholic days. I know it is absolutely tough to go through sobriety to end up with someone who partakes in drinking. She is a recovering alcoholic so being around liquor has to be hard and frustrating when you are stressed and want to have a drink too.

Before leaving my room she said, "Guess who I saw today? You remember my ex-boyfriend Leonard? I saw his little brother Dee today when I was buying cigarettes from the corner store. They moved out here from Alabama. Remember you used to stay with them? I'm sure you'll see him around. Anyway, I love you Nae Nae. I'm about to eat, shower and go to bed, girl." She closed the door and I laid in my bed thinking about Alabama.

Fuck Alabama and fuck Dee! My memories began to unfold what I tried to suppress. When I graduated from Kindergarten and we lived with Scarlet my mom fell in love with this guy named Leonard. The pressure of raising a child and living in the hood weighed her down. As most women do in those circumstances of being a single mother in the hood, they find love in the worst places. Or shall I say look for love in the wrong places. Either way you try to decipher their behavior, children get replaced by a falsehood of love to take their place. Most think we can fill voids with something or someone that is not the best for us. Yet we continue the endless cycle. Loneliness trumps responsibility, and temporary affection blossoms into toxicity. Her new found love soon led to my demise. Shortly after their boyfriend and girlfriend union, arrangements were made for me, her unbearable responsibility. In a blink of an eye I was sent on a plane to go live with his mother, brother, and sister in Prichard, Alabama.

Airplane rides were never my favorite. First off, it is scary to be so high in the air. Second, I was always traveling by myself. Most of me, always ended up at a destination. The other part of me resided in the previous location. I never helped to decide to live with people who knew me, but didn't really know me. The house looked huge but appeared smaller on the inside. I guess the large area of land surrounding the house made it appear that way. The walls had a dark wood siding on the inside and there were 3 bedrooms. Not only was the home peculiar, the people were very odd to me too. Everyone had a country accent so I had to decipher what they were saying all the time. Typical southern country bumpkin lingo. I was only 6 years old and not accustomed to different dialects.

People forget sometimes that children's opinions are valid because they aren't adults. I wasn't pleased with the move because the people I went to live with were complete strangers. I was on the opposite side of the country at a new house, beginning a new grade, going to a new school all alone! I came all the way to live in Alabama to sleep on the fucking couch.

I tried to make the best of it. Lynn's mother was nice and she cooked great food. The great food was the best part about it. I was always getting my hair hot combed which hurt because it felt like my scalp was on fire. I didn't have friends to play with because the kids that lived in the home were older. I hated school. The teachers were mean and still utilized corporal punishment. I was terrified of the school. I was in first grade and everything was new to me. I was whooped with a large wooden paddle with holes drilled into it, for talking while the teacher was talking.

My ass hurt for days! Before the first day of school started, I would walk with Lynn's little brother on long journeys to a Rec Center. I enjoyed going there because there were things to do. All day I played board games, sports, and ate a horrible free lunch.

***

Damn I thought as I laid in bed. I was always moving and shit. My life fucking sucked. I drifted off to sleep watching tv. That night I had an awful nightmare. I was walking down a dark hallway coming from the bathroom and went to lay down on a burgundy floral colored couch. I laid quietly trying to get warm nestling under the heavy blanket. I could hear little feet running around in the kitchen and got scared because I knew they belonged to the huge rat I had seen many times. Going to bed was never peaceful.

In my dream, I fell asleep and was awakened by a manly figure sitting next to me touching me inappropriately. Clenching the brown comforter that was over my body, I tucked the excess material of the blanket between my legs to shut out his prying hands. I kept pushing his hand away as his fingers touched my private, once he successfully bypassed the covers. I cringed and felt so uncomfortable. My private burned then and even after his fingers touched the lips of my vagina. I could smell his body odor. Dee reeked of sweat and dirt. I wanted to scream and tears fell down my face. I tried and tried at every touch by pushing back and even trying to get up. It didn't work. Every time I pushed his hand back it abruptly returned, until he was tired of quietly fighting to touch my young and innocent body. It was hard to fight him off all of the time.

Persistently Dee would be successful when I was asleep. The wooden panels in the living room created a darkness to hide what usually happened most nights. The faint sounds of dripping water in the bathroom and tiny patter of feet from the roommate of rats drowned out the tiny battles that happened in the dark.

Sitting up I glanced around my room focusing on how loud the volume of the tv was. I stumbled to the television and turned the power off. I sat on the edge of the bed with my head down. My nightmare seemed so real as if it was happening again. I walked to my room door and pushed it closed, turning the lock simultaneously. The clock read 4:00 am and I was nowhere sleepy or ready to go back to bed after reliving a horrible experience in my life.

Was that the reason I blocked out his entire existence? Is he another reason why I hate boys? Did I dress like a boy so guys wouldn't find me attractive? My brain was overwhelmed with thoughts. Am I a bad person because I never told anyone? I felt embarrassed, I'm never telling anyone I thought. I got dressed and packed my backpack getting ready for school.

The sun came up and there was a tiny knock at my room door. I smiled ear to ear when I pulled my room door open. "What's up little nicca?" I said to my step brother. My brother's little hoarse voice made my day and ended my sad moment when I saw his little peanut head and hazel eyes. He stood at the door and quickly stepped in, shaking two cigarettes in his hand. "Mama left her cigarettes on the kitchen table. You know what time it is!" I grabbed my backpack and followed him through the hallway, into his room, and out the sliding door into the backyard. We stood in silence smoking the cigarettes almost in unison with every puff. The silence was broken when we heard his dad call out his name. I gave him dap and jogged out the side gate trying to hurry so I wouldn't be seen or miss the school bus.

I loved my little brother. He was my step dad's son and wasn't my biological brother. The tiny truth of separate DNA, did not stop us from doing everything together. Despite his young age we always hung out. We mowed lawns, turned in recycling, and did anything to make money. We fixed bikes and rode our bikes anywhere they would take us until the sun went down. We even played video games together too. Our competitive personalities made us battle each other in football and basketball like complete strangers. Afterwards we would laugh about it and be friends again like nothing ever happened. Something about him was so genuine. He is always right on time with making me feel better without even knowing it. I loved that he could always positively improve my feelings without trying or having an ulterior motive.

CHAPTER 7

My first memory of me being alive was when I was around two or three years old. I lived in an apartment in Sunnyvale, California with my mom and my dad. The living room was large with a white cement fireplace. The kitchen was huge with a dining area and a glass sliding door that led out to the walkway to other apartments. There were 4 rooms in the apartment. My parents room of course was the master bedroom with an adjoining bathroom. My room was smaller and furnished with Strawberry Shortcake bedspread and toys. My uncle Andrew had his own room but I don't remember the contents of it. Last there was a room that belonged only to my dad, his own version of a man cave.

Whenever my dad wasn't home I would always sneak inside his man cave just to look at everything he collected and stored inside. The room's content consisted of a bar, a pair of tan bongos, hi tech stereo equipment and even bar signs on the walls. He had a tall lava lamp, made from an alcohol bottle, that stood on a metal frame and had a spout. Nothing ever came out when I would turn the spout. Yes, I tried several times. There were autographed pictures of Prince, Sammy Davis Jr., Michael Jackson and other famous stars on the walls. My dad stood next to the famous person in most of the pictures. Dark colored curtains hung over the large window blocking out any sunlight. He had an amazing stereo system with tall speakers and a lot of other boxes attached to control the sounds more intricately. My favorite part of the room was his collection of Albums in the carts on the floor. I would thumb through them and look at the various artists and designs. I would pretend to sing as I made beats with his wooden tambourines, banging them against my tiny hands. When everything was in its proper place I would sneak out, closing the door behind me.

I was always an observant child and would rummage through any and everything when left alone. I never took anything and just wanted to inspect and learn about what I observed. The majority of the time I spent at home I was accompanied by my uncle Andrew and my father too when he wasn't working. My dad was always cooking and he was the best cook. The food he cooked would melt in my mouth when we would eat after he effortlessly slaved in the kitchen. Sometimes my grandparents would visit and bring delicious food in Tupperware bowls. Those days were the best and we were all happy.

My father was an accountant for Atari. I remember when he brought a prototype of the game system home for my uncle. My uncle was so excited. Neither of us had seen anything like it before. My father removed the black machine out of the box and slowly followed the controllers and games. He confidently bragged how his friend only gave him an Atari game system to try out at home. Staring in awe he connected it to the television and we waited attentively for him to power it up.

When the game system came on it wasn't like anything we had ever seen. My uncle and I had been to arcades before, having one in our home made us feel special. I watched and listened closely when my father gave instructions on how to use the strange device. Hours quickly passed by with all of our eyes glued to the television and I don't even think my father cooked dinner. He had never missed a night cooking for us and tonight was the first. Our souls were full of excitement and happiness. Lost in a new Era of Atari video gaming.

Our hour of giddiness was interrupted by the sliding door closing loudly in the kitchen. My dad quickly turned the Atari system off with a push of his finger. All too familiar with what awaited in the near future my uncle grabbed my hand guiding me to my room. He sat me on my bed gesturing for me to sit tight. He disappeared in the hallway and I momentarily heard running water. Coming back to my room he gathered up my pajamas and guided me to the bathroom.

Bending down to check the water he told me to get undressed and get in the tub, and closed the door behind him as he walked out the bathroom. I sat in the tub and my novice behavior of bathing showed at every thud when I dropped soap loudly into the tub. I could hear muffled sounds yelling and swearing behind the closed bathroom door but it didn't bother me. My mom and dad argue all the time. He complained of how she was never home and always going to happy hour. I didn't understand why he was mad. Who wouldn't want to be happy? Wasn't that what Happy Hour was for, to make people happy? I think he should go to happy hour and maybe he wouldn't be so mad all the time.

My uncle poked his head in and told me to get out and get dressed, disappearing again behind the door. I followed his instructions drying off quickly because it felt like the wind was blowing on my wet body. After I dried off I put on my pajamas and I was having a difficult time. I didn't dry off too well and the clothes were sticking to my body not allowing me to put them on properly.

My tiny muscles hurt and ached from the tugging and pulling, I was relieved when I finished.

Grabbing my dirty clothes I walked towards the bathroom door and it swung open before I could grab the door knob. My heart dropped and so did the clothes in my hand when I saw the disfigured face on the front of the The Dramatics' album cover. It's lifelike distorted face seemed to protrude in 3D, towards my face as my uncle waved the album back and forth bringing the picture to life. The squinting eye winked at me, I screamed at the top of my lungs at the horrific album cover. I always avoided the stack of Albums where I knew the album was hidden. Yet it always found its way into my uncle's hands when he wanted a good laugh at scaring the hell out of me.

My scream unintentionally broke up the argument between my mom and dad. I wonder if showing me the album to make me scream was part of my uncle's plan to bring their cycle of dysfunctional communication to an end? If so, he was smarter than I thought he was. I didn't like the album cover or the 4 horns on that demon, but I loved my uncle!

CHAPTER 8

The first time I visually saw and was scared of a monster was the demonic figure placed upon the album cover of the Dramatics titled the Dramatic Experience. The irony of its album title defined how I felt when I laid eyes upon its artistic ability to stand out. Till this day my heart rate accelerates and skips a beat at the very sight or thought of it. The disfigured eyes, the many horns, the disproportion of how its facial figures line up on its faces lingers in the depths of my mind. This image stuck with me throughout my wonderful childhood making monsters my kryptonite. The album cover persuaded my belief that monsters appear to be physically repulsive and fearful. In no way did I ever imagine monsters were disguised as regular people. All the other monsters I encountered came to me in the dark and tore me apart without killing me. The first time I saw a monster in real life he appeared to be a well dressed young man with the intentions of having a great time.

My best friend Matty was a year older than my cousin and I. Everyone thought she was amazing and her character led her to be one of the most popular girls in our neighborhood and at our high school. Her presence made me feel invincible when I was around her because everyone was always drawn to her bold personality. Instantaneously Marty was added to my circle of friends. The first time my cousin Kesha and I saw her, was when she sitting outside her home on Fordham street on the back of her uncle's burgundy El Camino truck. Her legs swung back and forth and we noticed her blue Nike Air Max before she opened her mouth. She wore a new black hoodie and black basketball shorts and two pairs of fresh bone white Nike socks. Matty' charismatic voice drew us in when she said "Hi" to us in her San Franciscan accent. From that day on we were thick as thieves and could always be found hanging out together.

Everyday we did the same thing and our routine rarely ever changed. We met up at Matty' house in the morning and made a sandwich to take with us to school. She always had the expensive bologna, cheese, and Home Pride Wheat Bread that deliciously went well together. Once she was dressed we walked to the school bus stop and waited in the cold morning air for the raggedy yellow school bus. We traveled the long 30 minute ride on the cold shaking school bus to Woodside High School. Everyday we were yelled at by the angry bus driver for breaking the rules. Matty was a rule breaker and a complete rebel. Most days the bus driver would pull over just for Matty sitting on her knees in the seat, for her hitting one of the boys, or chewing gum on the bus. Following the complaint of the rule breaking, Matty would curse the bus driver out.

Routinely the bus driver would pull the bus over and we would sit for what seemed like eternity until everyone stopped laughing and eventually was late to school. No one ever got mad at Matty for causing us to be late to school, she was actually praised for who and what she did.

After school we would go to Matty' house and wait for her aunty to leave for church, so we could smoke a blunt. Matty always had weed from one of the many drug dealers she was friends with or dating in the neighborhood. Kesha and I would wonder when she had time to talk to all these guys because we were always together. Today was different, she didn't have any weed. What, no weed! The walls of happiness crumbled into an amber like fire around our hopes of smoking our troubles away. Kesha laughed in awe at our addict-like behaviors because she didn't smoke weed and didn't care for it. Shaking her head with her lips twisted in an awkward sideways position she blurted out, "Y'all bitches are some fiends!" Matty and I glared at her. I thought about how I just rode my raggedy ten speed all the way from the Mid just to smoke and there was no stash. "Fuck" I thought, "I could have went to the Rec instead." Dee began hanging out in the Mid after our first encounter. I would see him way too much than I wanted to, so as a result I had begun hanging out in the Village. I figured the more I hung out in a different turf I could avoid running into him. Plus I began smoking blunts more too, and Matty always had weed.

Matty and I sat in silence as we watched Kesha disappear around the corner when she passed the gates that led into Costano Elementary. The silence was broken when her older brother walked up moving quickly as if someone was following him. He smelled of cologne and was well dressed like Matty in the latest designer jeans and new Nike Tennis shoes probably from one of the stores in San Francisco. His accent was similar to Matty and he walked coolly past us with his pants sagging lower than I had ever seen before. It was my first time meeting her older brother before and I only met her younger brother who still lived in SF.

Matty trailed behind him and I followed her into the house. I waited for a while in the living room and I could hear her asking him for a blunt. In a blink of an eye she appeared from the hallway and we went back outside in the front yard.

Instantly I asked, "So what did he say?".

With disapproval she said, "He's going to smoke with us, with his stingy ass." I replied, "shoot well that's cool, at least we get to smoke. Right?".

"I guess.", she said. "I wanted my own blunt. I'm not trying to wait on him to cut his D up, then roll a blunt and smoke. That's gone take forever!" she huffed, rolling her eyes.

Matty wasn't lying, the wait was long and we sat in the front yard until the sun was almost going down. Her brother slammed the door and skipped out to the front yard with a fat Philly blunt in his ear. I dropped my head when I saw it because it was so fat I thought we still had to wait until he rolled the blunt. In a quick smooth movement he took the blunt out of his ear. Stroking the lighter with his thumb, he inhaled and exhaled, blowing the huge cloud of smoke out. He pulled part of the smoke up his nose slowly, showing he was an expert smoker. Passing the blunt to Matty he walked off down the street heading to the back of the Village probably to see one of the girls he courted. Females were his only business in the back of the

Village Neighborhood. Matty and I passed the blunt back and forth to each other. I coughed more than usual because the potency of the weed was entirely stronger than any weed I had ever smoked in my life.

Unaware of traveling into the house, I surprisingly woke up laying on Matty's bed. I could tell from the crack in the curtains that it was dark and the sun had long gone down. When the fuck did I go to sleep? I didn't remember going to sleep. I wiped my sweaty forehead pondering on when did I ever come inside the house and lay down? Upon wiping my forehead my hand grazed my hair and what used to be a flat ironed wrap style was now a nest of sweaty tangled hair. "Ugh, are you kidding me?", I said to myself. I sat up and my head began to spin and pound at the same time. Feeling immediately nauseous, I lifted myself slowly off the bed and struggled to stand upright. Matty wasn't anywhere to be found in the house. So I grabbed my sweater and headed for the front door.

I made eye contact with Sam, their overgrown German Shepherd and he watched as I struggled to go through the front door and screen door without slamming it. I tried to avoid making a lot of noise because her aunty was usually in her room reading her bible. No way did I want to socially interact with her, in my current condition. The cold air hit me in the face and made me feel somewhat refreshed. After a few seconds my scalp and head was very cold from the dampness of my hair. I could hear a car motor running across the street from Matty house, and I recognized the car from around the neighborhood. I didn't remember who drove it but I was certain she was probably sitting in the passenger seat of its muscle car frame.

I walked to the side of the yard to retrieve my ten speed, relieved I didn't have to walk home. I picked up the weightless frame and headed down the driveway towards the sidewalk. I ran on the side of the bike to get a head start before jumping up on it, to take off riding. My body shook the bike frame a little causing the front wheel to shake, and I heard a loud sound as the wheel rim hit the concrete. "Oh no!" I thought, "Not now, not a flat tire!" I recited every curse word I knew in my head and some aloud under my breath. I hopped off the bike and walked beside it as I pushed it. I heard a voice yell from across the street even though I couldn't make out who it was. "My bad, I rode your bike and caught a flat!", said the familiar voice. I recognized the voice and it was raspy with a San Franciscan accent, Harold. Harold was Matty's younger brother. When the fuck did he get to town. He rarely visited and what a way to make an entrance by getting a flat tire on my bike. Ugh, what an asshole. I was beginning to get the impression Matty's whole family was poisoned.

    I stopped at the corner to reposition my grip on the bike because it was starting to tilt weirdly in a diagonal lean due to the flat tire. A car pulled up beside me and out hopped Matty grinning ear to ear. "Awe blood, my bad about the bike. My brother Harold flattened the tire when he rode it to the back of the Village.", she muttered. I remained quiet, too angry to respond. My first thought was buried in the back of mind, under all the curse words I was currently thinking. I was a little relieved that she came to walk me halfway home like she normally did, because it was so dark and I was terrified of the dogs that roamed the streets in the Village. The silence was broken when she apologized again.

    "Umm, you apologized already shit! I'm just glad you didn't leave me hanging." I said thankfully. I tried to manage not to drop the bike. My equilibrium was totally off and my head had begun to spin again.

    "No," Matty began quietly. "I wasn't apologizing for the bike. I was apologizing for my brother giving us a grimy blunt."

    "What the fuck is a grimy blunt? No wait, did his punk ass lace the weed in the blunt? No, no, no! You gotta be fucking kidding me!" I blurted out, finally losing my temper in a rage.

    "My bad blood, my bad for real. I wouldn't have let you smoke it if I knew. Promise blood that's the truth." Matty said, looking for some type of response. I didn't respond, I kept walking. I barely looked at the cars that approached us, as I crossed the street on University. I didn't say goodbye or look back to acknowledge her existence or her apology. It seemed as if my body was floating. I took the shortcut cutting through the Library parking lot and across the dry field to Bay Road. My anger really fueled me because my long walk up Bay Road briefly flew by, as I turned the corner onto Ralmar Street.

Not caring about the dusty road ruining my Nike shoes, I drug my feet up the street running out of strength to push the bike. I finally walked into my yard and dropped the bike on the side of the house not caring how it fell to the ground. I pushed the side gate open leading to the backyard and drug my feet across the leaf ridden concrete. I quickly pushed my bedroom window open to avoid anyone catching me in the backyard. I used the crate outside my window to give me a boost up. I crawled through the dusty and paint chipped window seal being careful enough to avoid getting a splinter. Closing the window I fell back onto my bed, kicking my shoes off simultaneously. My eyes fell shut, and my whole body cringed with pain.

I heard a tap at my room door and before I could respond, it opened. My eyes tried to focus in the darkness but it was impossible. The click of the light came after the light blinded me leaving me covering my eyes.

"Where have you been sis?"

said the little raspy voice. "oh, you're asleep," he said.

Although the light blinded the hell out of me, I was relieved when he came in and sat on the edge of the bed. He didn't talk anymore, he just turned my TV on. He pushed the power button to my video game and began playing in silence.

I don't remember what time I drifted off to sleep. I felt like shit when my alarm went off sounding like the bells that rang for a fire in a fire station. Barely lifting my body I pulled myself out of bed and grabbed my clothes heading to the bathroom to take a shower. I reminisced about the bad dream I had and was happy it was over when I woke up. After drying myself off and getting dressed I wiped the mirror so I could do my hair. I jumped in terror when I saw how my hair looked. How in the hell did my hair get like this? No, no, no, I wasn't dreaming! That bitch Matty brother fucking laced the weed! Grabbing my hair brush I threw my hair into a quick ponytail. "Oh it's on now!", I thought. I grabbed my backpack rushing out the front door so I wouldn't be late to school.

CHAPTER 9

Weirdly my mind drifted to how long it had been since I spoke to or hung out with Matty while I was waiting at the bus stop. Not that I cared. I often thought about a lot of things that happened or could happen. Most of the time I would overwork my brain. I always focused on the negative and sometimes would experience panic attacks when I would think too much. Months had passed since I hung out with Matty. During our departure, I returned my interest and focus to school.

One of the things I did was try out for the basketball team at the Boys and Girls Club in Menlo Park. I surprised myself by landing a guard position on the team. I'm sure she didn't care that I hadn't hung out with her either. Matty's youngest brother had moved to East Palo Alto and was now attending Woodside High School. I was easily replaced by her new best friend, the ever so charmingly Harold. The two of them were thick as thieves, and were hardly seen apart. Matty and her brother Harold were collectively terrible. They caused so much trouble at school! Witnessing their destruction of any and everything around them my level of avoiding her, to skyrocket into the stratosphere!

The wind wrapped around my ankles and up my legs causing me to shiver. I rubbed my frail little brown hands together trying to get warm. Peering through my watery eyes I looked for the yellow bus to come over the overpass on the other side of the 101 freeway entrance.

"Ugh", I thought, "this bus is taking forever!"

I shifted my weight back and forth on each foot trying to warm up but it wasn't working. I hated the Bay area weather. The sun was rising yet it was so damn cold! Every time I breathed out the steam caused my glasses to fog up.

The cold morning air and slight wind made me focus so intensely on the weather. I was so distracted that I was completely unaware that the school bus had crept up and came to a halt in front of me. I hopped on quickly barely allowing the doors to completely open. The irony of me heading to the back of the bus sunk in when I realized the heater on the bus was closest to the front. Everyone at my stop piled onto the bus as I secured my spot in the second to the last seat on the left. I glanced at the rip on the back of the seat to briefly double check that this was indeed my seat. I scooted my backpack to the far end of my seat to represent "don't sit by me", indirectly. My bus stop was the first stop of the route and I had plenty of time to get my "don't sit by me" face together.

The bus slowly pulled away from the curb jerking, as the bus driver struggled with changing the gears due to the cold. Intuition told me to glance out the foggy back window. Sure enough I saw a tall figure running towards the bus wildly waving his arms trying to flag the bus down.

"Wait, someone else is coming!", I yelled.

The bus driver slammed on the brakes and everything not braced down, flew to the floor when the bus came to a quick stop. The doors squeaked as they opened and Mason was on the bus in one stride due to his long legs. His big eyes focused on me and was followed by a nod of approval knowing I influenced the bus driver to wait for him. His big bodily frame trudged down the aisle and he plopped down in the seat opposite of me.

"What up Nae?", he said in his deep voice. He smelled of CK cologne and baked goods, nothing unusual. Mason was dressed in the latest Jordan shoes and Nike gear. Reaching over he handed me a tiny white bag and I knew its contents was filled with blueberry donut holes, my favorite.

Routinely I reached in my backpack and handed him the assignments for English and History class.

"Right on," he said, skimming through the papers checking the finished product. Closing the deal he reached in his pocket and pulled out a twenty dollar bill.

"I did it like you said and switched up the handwriting and changed up the answers so you won't get caught." I said to reassure his thoughts of possibly getting caught.

"I'm not tripping", he said "I trust you."

The bus took what seemed like forever to go through the bus route. With all the chatting and sports talk I drifted off to sleep. When I opened my eyes I was in a room that was very familiar. I glanced around at the brightly lit television displaying the latest version of Super Mario Brothers. Yoshi ran around wildly in circles making the funny popping sound when he ran into anything.

Duh, it was my friend's Katina house.

I slung my feet to the floor tripping over the newly styled Nintendo controllers almost pulling the brand new system to the floor. Pushing it back onto the dresser I slowly opened the room door. Walking past tons of hoarded junk in the hallway I made it swiftly to the bathroom.

Without getting caught in the awkward back and forth of who was going to pass first due to the limited amount of space in the hallway, I closed the bathroom door behind me. I used the bathroom and returned to lay down in the extra twin bed in her room. I laid down and the spot was still warm, and I snuggled warmly under? I was used to her laying in the same bed as me. Normally one of the twin beds is covered with all her name brand clothes she had. Most of the time we would end up falling asleep anyway on the same bed. This time it was different. IN the past we would sleep at opposite ends of the bed, but oddly she snuggled up towards my back. Scared to move, I laid still. I was glad it wasn't so cold anymore.

About an hour later I woke up to the sounds of subtle whispers faintly in my ear. The warm air that followed each whisper made every hair on my body rise. The light voice tickled my ear.

Every word made my body feel tingly. I finally made out what the soft girly voice said, "Touch me right here." Katina guided my hand to her breast and I caressed her soft breast reluctantly enjoying it. She moaned as she moved towards me. We finally came within reach for her to kiss me slowly as I caressed her breast. Immediately I began thinking this was wrong. Thereafter I felt it to be natural and right. My body melted all over! We kissed passionately, making my body temperature rise. I had kissed a boy before and it felt awkward. With her, kissing felt amazing!

Out of this world even. I didn't mind being different. Now I didn't mind being from another planet either.

Expertly without breaking the rhythm she moved my hand from her soft skin down towards her stomach. I stopped there and basked in the moment of how firm and soft her skin was momentarily guiding one finger around her belly button with one finger. Briefly she stopped kissing me and buried her face into the nape of my neck and moaned softly into my ear. Her hand gripped my hand and she continued towards her underwear sliding our hands into her love spot. Once my hand was there, I froze. I was unaware of what to do. I had never been with a girl sexually. She pushed my hand over her love spot and our hands moved as one in a circular motion. Her tiny short hairs prickled the inside of hand. With her hand on top of mine she pressed my middle finger forward, and pushed my finger in between her moist lips. It was like nothing I had ever done before. My hand was very wet as if she had wet herself but the texture was thicker and very slippery. Once my finger was inside her she continued to kiss me wildly.

Moving her waist in circular motions she shivered weirdly, and fell asleep in my arms.

Gasping for air I lifted my head up from the top of my backpack resting on my lap. Slobber slung onto my arm and I tried to catch it with my jacket sleeve, to avoid embarrassment of anyone seeing me. Looking around everyone was still chit chatting amongst themselves and the sound of the turn signal overpowered their conversations with a loud clicking sound. The bus stood in the long line of cars occupying the left turn lane leading into the high school.

I remembered I laid there not knowing what to do or say. When we awoke the next day, what happened was never spoken of or discussed as if it never happened. Our secret routinely happened most nights when I would spend the night over her house, always initiated by her. Every time was always better than the last and I grew more experienced with her each time. One weekend without notice she stopped returning my calls and we stopped hanging out completely. When people spoke of her they talked about how happy she was with her new boyfriend. I know for sure I wasn't in love with her because it didn't bother me that she had a boyfriend. I just missed the familiarity of having a place to hang out and someone to have fun with. We had done everything together! We took pictures, went out to eat, traveled, went to the movies, and even went shopping millions of times.

A couple of years have passed since I last saw her. When we would see one another, the vibe was always dry. She acted as if she never knew me when our paths would cross. My loyalty would show when I pretended with her. Why was she so distant as if I initiated the encounters we experience? I'm sure she was trying to forget me completely and forget what happened. I mean shit we were only 14 and being gay was not accepted in the society we live in. People were known to be disowned by family and friends for liking the same sex.

I did my best everyday to try and be girly. I hate girl clothes and they were uncomfortable. Thank God for TLC because they made it acceptable to wear baggy boy clothes. As far as anyone knew I was currently being trendy with my clothes selections. I didn't care for boys, I mean if a guy was cute or handsome I had no reason to deny that. There was never the attraction I had for a girl. I don't know if I tried to have boyfriends but it was so mediocre. Nothing made my blood boil how she did. No one ever came close.

I grabbed my backpack and slung it across my back, straightening my clothes as I stood up on the bus. Shaking my head remembering how good I felt when I was with her I headed slowly toward the forming line of people exiting the bus. I felt someone tap my shoulder from behind me. I jumped, turning around quickly, staring at his chest. I looked upward at his dark chocolate face. "What are you smiling at Nae?", said Mason. "I was smiling, just thinking how imma kick your but in basketball at lunch!", I said charmingly as I exited the bus.

CHAPTER 10

I was flourishing! Basketball was going great! I was the wingman to Lacy, the best female basketball player from East Palo Alto and Menlo Park combined. My social life was at an all time high and I was no longer just Markesha's cousin, Caroline or Little Chester sister. I was my own person creating my own identity. People often experience some type of loss when their life is getting better or they become successful at what they inspire to be. It was no surprise, when I lost a big part of me that I would remember forever.

 I was looking for love in all the wrong places. After my rendezvous with Katina, I was determined to forget it all and give boys a try despite my negative feelings about them. Everyday I passed the little dirty green house up the street from my house. Music played loudly and the group of guys stood with pride by there nicely painted cars, engrossed in conversations of money, sex, and drugs. I would drop my head and tuck my basketball tightly under my arm gliding pass like a low flying aircraft. They all stood in awe when I passed, complimenting my new shoes or making comments about how good I was in basketball. They would say anything to get my attention, but I never gave mine.

 One day after school my step sister called me out to the porch. I had no reason why she was calling me, because she never let a day go by without showing how much she disliked me. Her hatred was never blatant. It was hidden underneath and intertwined in sneaky misfortunes I always experienced when she was involved in the equation. I was smart enough to catch on to it and kept my distance from her. Nonetheless without thought I pushed the heavy white metal screen door open, only to be blindly bombarded by her once again.

"This is Corey, Darnel's friend. He wanted to talk to you.", she said with a Chester cat smirk on her face.

Without any thought I quickly responded, "Don't you live down the street? You see me everyday and now you wanna talk to me?" Cory stood staring with his big brown eyes, speechless about what to say next. I looked at him and shook my head, retracting my hand allowing the screen door to slam as I stepped back into the threshold.

Cory tried everyday to talk to me. He tried when he would see me at Shop N Go, the Rec, or passing his house. I admired his persistence, so I finally gave in to him. We became friends, extending our friendship to watching TV or shooting hoops in my backyard. He wasn't very good at basketball. I began letting him win after I saw I was better than him. I got tired of winning. I stopped trying just so he could win when we would play 21 or Hunch. Cory was really nice and seemed like he liked me for me and not to just have sex. It felt nice to be around someone that didn't have ulterior motives.

I was coasting through our friendship, and hung out with him when I wasn't playing basketball. One day I felt a spark that led to me having sex with him, when my mom and step dad weren't home. They planned a trip to gamble at a new casino that all their friends gloated about winning a lot of money. The experience didn't last long and I didn't feel as amazing as I did when I was with Katina. I felt good temporarily and my short gratification landed me in a place I didn't want to be!

My head was spinning as I sat in my favorite seat on the back of the bus. I gobbled down the blueberry donut holes Mason gave me before the bus reached the second stop of our route. I coughed and coughed and thought about how I hated to have a cold. My chest felt heavy, my throat hurt, and I had about the same energy I would have after a basketball tournament! I sat quietly daydreaming about laying down when I got home because despite it being 6:30 in the morning, I felt as if I hadn't slept at all.

I was extremely hungry by lunchtime. I was first in line at the new, wooden, octagon shaped kiosk, Woodside built in the Senior patio to buy 2 Jumbo Jacks with cheese. I ate them with no hesitation followed by my favorite bag of Lay's Sour Cream and Onion chips. My huge lunch gave me the energy I needed to make it through 5th period. 6th period flew by quickly. I awoke when the dismissal bell rang, so I'm sure it was due to me being asleep. I slept through the entire 6th period? No Bueno!

I slept the entire bus ride home. I drug my feet across the pavement down Bay Road and across the millions of rocks on my street. My journey came to an end as I fell through an imaginary pack of clouds when I dropped backwards onto my bed. I was awakened by my mother's voice demanding that I take a pregnancy test. I didn't have any fight in me, I was too tired to rebuttal any demands she had. I was asleep through her interrogation, the blood test, and came back to life when the nurse practitioner acclaimed me pregnant!

No fucking way, I thought to myself. My mom was reluctantly nurturing and asked what I wanted to do. I wasn't keeping this baby I thought to myself. I wasn't ruining my chances of going to the WNBA by having a child with someone I pretended to be in love with. No Love and Basketball for me!

Psyching myself out with how much I didn't want a baby, everything changed the moment I opened the car door of my mom's yellow Biarritz Cadillac the day of my abortion. The intimidating muster of people flooded the parking lot of the Redwood City Planned Parenthood Clinic with huge signs of dead aborted babies. My stomach was in knots and my cautiousness now had a voice of reason. I couldn't kill a child! When I pondered over my future actions, that is exactly what I was about to do. I was taking a life, so I could have one. I felt selfish. I knew what I was about to do was inhumane. I continued to think if I went through with my mission, would I be able to live with myself?

Once taken to my examination room, I undressed slowly and got into the gown provided by the nurse. I took my time folding my clothes and placed them in a tiny pile on the vacant chair next to the examination table. In the corner of the room stood a complex machine, with clear tubing and multiple buttons. Cold air embraced my body as I waited impatiently, swinging my legs back and forth in a nervous fashion. Before I knew it, I was lying on a cold table in an operation room. The doctors moved quickly around the cold room, stopping to hook me to an IV and prepping me for one of the most important decisions in my life.

What was I doing?, I began to think. What seemed like the easiest thing to do, was making me feel terrible, and was the hardest. It would be easy to abort the baby and go on living the life I was destined to live. So why was it so hard to do? The decision I was making was sure to come back and haunt me. Well everyone who kills someone is always haunted, right? Was I really committing a murder? My eyelids began to get heavy as I started to panic and regret my decision. Tears fell slowly from the corner of my eyes and picked up speed as each second passed. One of the doctors saw me crying and made me feel lower than low. "Huh, huh girl none of that crying. You wasn't crying when you was having sex!" the nurse spoke sternly. "Plus crying causes your sinuses to clog up and we don't need you having complications while you're under the knife!". I cried even more as my eyes finally closed and everything went black.

CHAPTER 11

There's a difference in being mad at yourself and hating yourself and I think I was feeling a combination of the two. Being mad at yourself I find to be temporary and there is a willing attitude to forgive yourself and learn from your mistakes you have made. Hating yourself is a long drawn out process of feeling regret with a sprinkle of disgust and depression. Having an abortion at a young age not only disposed of an unwanted fetus but depreciated my soul to the most miniscule spirit that ever existed. I was embellished in depression and felt lost because I had no one to express my true feelings with. At school the teachers and my peers thought I was amazing. Despite my small hiccup of getting pregnant my mother thought I was an awesome daughter. I never gave my mother any trouble, unlike my step brother and sister. My almost future baby daddy had me on a pedal stool; I wasn't sure if it was due to his relief of me eliminating the responsibility of a baby or if he really liked me. Why couldn't I see what they saw in me? I knew I was an exceptional person, nonetheless I did not feel like one!

I spent most of my days after school in my room, not having the desire to play basketball or hang out. The new hobby I picked up was poetry and writing rap songs. It was a great hobby and I became good at it. My huge collection of cds provided a foundation of endless instrumentals to write to. Writing became my outlet and it was an easy way to express myself. Speaking and talking wasn't one of my stronger personality traits, so I hid within the words of my notebook creations. Writing was therapeutic and my recurrence of losing something when I gained something awaited within the shadows of my spontaneous combustion of a life.

My sister began to grow fond of my existence and we started to hang out more than usual. Did she actually like me or were we the living phrase that misery loves company? Who knows?

Sulking in my regretful decisions I was around the house more than normal and I became more obtainable. From time to time she would grace me with her presence, wandering into my room unannounced. I was always on alert with her. I knew part of the fact she wanted to hang out was she wanted to woo the likings of my boyfriend's best friend, Darnel. She played hard to get with him and smothered me to gain information about him from Cory. I would always just tell her that I know he likes her so why is she so mean towards him. Like every other time he was mentioned she would randomly change the subject, which I found weird. I would think to myself if you like him why would you change the subject if you currently started the topic of discussion about him. Her thought process was too complex, even for me. Talking with her was exhausting and always drained what little energy I was willing to give her.

One day after having an exceptional day at school I wandered into the house feeling great. I was partially over my depressing slump and felt good overall. The bullshit lingered in the air like the smell of butt in a public bathroom. My naive behavior didn't allow me to smell what awaited me. I walked in the front door making my way down the long hallway and dropped my backpack on the floor. My stomach started to growl. I returned to the front of the house to the small kitchen and glanced out the front window. Peering over the lemon tree in front of the window I looked left and right to see what I could see as I washed my hands. The scalding hot water stung my hands and I yanked them back quickly. Turning the cold water up higher I rinsed the soap off. I twisted the left knob and turned off the sink shaking my hands to wave the water off them.

I opened up the fridge, bending down to get a closer look at the contents. I got lost in all the leftovers, as my eyes scanned all the shelves. I grabbed one of the bowls containing some leftover spaghetti and stood upward to close the refrigerator. As I closed the refrigerator my eyes met my stepsister's evil light brown eyes. Startling me, I jumped almost dropping the heavy Tupperware bowl. "What the hell?" I said irritated at her sneaking around. "Where you trying to scare me and make me drop the bowl?" I said in an irritating voice. She stood staring at me as if I didn't say anything to her. I turned my back to her, breaking the zombie-like stare she had going with me. Her timing was weird but normal for her character.

"You know Cory went to juvie!" she said happily as if that was a good thing. I shook my head yes and continued to get my after school snack together, trying to ignore her dark presence in the kitchen. I walked around her and reached into the refrigerator and got a piece of kraft cheese.

Brushing passed her again I opened my sliced cheese and layed it like a blanket over the mound of spaghetti on my plate. Setting the microwave for two and a half minutes, I remembered my plate was still on the counter. I plopped it into the microwave slamming the door and pushed the start button. Her entire presence gave me chills and I was really starting to reject her company.

"Yea Cory is in juvie!" She started the one way conversation again. I just stared at her like "duh you said that already, and?" She lacked the reception of my obviously irritated body language. She began again, "Yea I was at my mom house and my cousin Debbie called from juvie on a collect call. She said she went out with Cory and they kissed during movie time. The boys and girls get to watch movies together. It's dark enough for couples to sneak in the back and make out without getting caught. Lucky you got an abortion right!" She stood in the kitchen waiting for a reaction and luckily the sound of the microwave beeping to an end broke the silence. A smirk was on her face and her light brown eyes shimmered, reminding me of the Cheshire Cat from Alice in Wonderland. Quickly I turned and grabbed my plate out of the microwave. I went to my room leaving her standing in the kitchen, probably plotting her next move. I locked my room door and sat on my bed weeping silently. The sound of the door knob turning made me stare at the door even though I knew it was locked.

ETERNAL BAGGAGE

Ok, I was officially done! Caroline delivered the news that finally prompted me to edge. Cory was lying to me all this time! He didn't really like me and he was messing around with someone else! Caroline enjoyed delivering the news to me too. She smiled and spoke the news as if it was a good thing to see me cringe at what she had to say. She knew I was being cheated on and probably her whole family knew too. If her family knew, did the whole Menlo Park know too.

Did everyone that was in juvie know too? I felt so humiliated and I wanted to die!

I hated boys and I hated my step sister! I looked at the bottle of Extra Strength Tylenol and knew that was the answer to my problems. I took everyone that was in the bottle without a second thought. I cried and cried waiting for the pills to take effect. My body temperature began to change and I shook the front of my shirt to cool myself down. I cracked my window and pushed it up high enough to crawl out. As I walked further into the back yard towards the back of the house my head began to spin. I felt as if I was on a twisty ride at the fair. Before I sat down on the brick flower bed I started to throw up profusely. I threw up until liquid was coming out my nose and my stomach tightened into a knot. I held my stomach as I coughed and gagged until nothing came out. My eyes grew heavy and I layed down in the backyard on the soft green grass.

***

No, I didn't die. I wanted to die or at least I thought I wanted to die. I awoke from my deep sleep feeling just as miserable as I did before I passed out. I don't think it was meant for me to die because I threw up everything I consumed that day, including the several Tylenol. I'm glad I didn't die and happy no one found me or knew what I tried to do. Ok I think that was by far the dumbest thing I have ever done in my life. I barely was over the abortion and I tried to eliminate myself. What an idiot! How could I let someone push me that far to take my own life? Caroline was very vindictive and pure evil!

CHAPTER 12

Evil sometimes manifests inside people without knowledge and sometimes it's learned and adapted due to the environment in which we live. My mother was one of the cases in which she learned how to be evil from those around her. She was always being lured into the webs of malicious people, naive to what was actually going on. Entrapped in a web of love and hate her body coiled into a massive cocoon. She eventually clawed her way out through the sticky intertwining strings and landed in a situation of neverending turmoil.

I was happy to be living with my mom. Summer couldn't have come at a better time because with her new apartment came the amenities of a huge pool. Her apartment was small and quaint but she made it her own with her plants and different trinkets she managed to hold onto from our house on Gonzaga Street. Her apartment also came with a new boyfriend. New people didn't bother me, as long as they didn't interfere with my program.

Petey was an ok guy. Sometimes he would watch me when my mom would go to work. He dressed nice and had a yellow pinto style car with loud music in it. I enjoyed listening to music as he drove around running errands and doing little odd and end jobs for people to make money. He always played NWA, Ice Cube, and any other rap music that was popular. I would nod my head as we went up and down almost every street in the 2.5 square miles of East Palo Alto.

Anytime I was hungry he would buy food or snacks for me, so I couldn't complain. He was cool in my book.

Like any other Friday night my mother relaxed from a long work week by indulging in her favorite pastime, drinking alcohol. She always spoke about the American Indian blood she possessed in her genes and how alcohol made her aggressive. The alcohol would manifest her into a whole nother person, opposite from her quiet timid self. No she didn't care that she would regret how she acted the next day. I think she admired her alter ego and thrived to live in the present moment of her drinking habit. Drinking allowed her to say, think, and act out her true feelings of when she was sober, because she didn't have the courage when she wasn't drinking. Nonetheless she was drinking and showing me attention so it didn't matter.

My mother played music and cleaned up around the house as she made small talk with me in passing, telling old stories that came to mind. I bobbed my head to the Miss You Much song by Janet Jackson and enjoyed her conversations while I colored in my coloring book. When I got bored of coloring I followed her back and forth through the small apartment. I watched her petite figure maneuver around cleaning up things that didn't really need cleaning.

I was in the bathroom when I heard the front door slam shut, followed by muffled sounds of arguing. Intrigued with the distant shouting, I came out of the bathroom. What seemed to be the front door was actually the room door shutting. The door was closed so roughly it left it slightly ajar from it not catching the latch. I peeped through the cracked door and saw my mother arguing with Petey. They both yelled obscenities and waved their hands back and forth displaying how intense they felt at the present moment. The arguing drowned out music that continued to play as if they placed a pillow over the speakers. I began to cough as the smoke from an unattended cigarette burned in the ashtray on the milk crate nightstand next to the bed. My mom looked in the direction of the room door catching sight of me. Attempting to end the argument she yelled, "I'm going out!" storming into the room, shutting the door behind her. Eyes filled with tears she whispered, "Sorry Nae-Nae. Put your coat and shoes on too, okay."

I hurried to do what she asked and sat on the bed, feeling the sense we were fleeing. I stuck my hands inside of the pockets of the noisy cold jacket I wore. The polyester material made my body cold and uncomfortable to get settled in gripping the back of my shoulders. I watched her pick out a blue dress from the closet and toss it on the bed. She handed me her car keys and told me to go wait in the car, assuring me she would be right out. Apprehensively I took the keys not wanting to leave her behind. My instincts told me to disagree with her demands but I was afraid to undermine her and make matters worse.

Forever was shorter than my wait in the car. The windows began to fog up during my wait and my mother never made it to the car. I stared at the door waiting for it to open, but it never did. A black Cadillac pulled up in the parking lot and my eyes were temporarily blinded by the bright head lights shining through the front windshield. I watched closely as a tall stalky figure approached the car, stopping on my side to tap on the window. Rolling the window down, I squinted at him trying to remember who the man was as familiarity filled my mind. "Willie!", I thought to myself. My mom's ex boyfriend. Why would he be here? What's going on, I thought. Where is my mom and why didn't she come out?

Moving quickly he told me to roll the window up and opened the car door. He reached across me and took the keys out of the ignition, guiding me to get out of the car. "Come with me Nae-Nae.", he said in his Barry White of a voice. He was so dark skinned and wore black so all I could see was the white of his eyes and his pearly white teeth. He closed the door as I got in his black Cadillac and disappeared for a couple mins. He came back to the car with my bags and this totally confused me, but I still didn't ask any questions. Oh well I thought and my eyes drifted off to sleep.

***

I could hear familiar voices when I woke up. It wasn't dark anymore and the bright sun blinded me as I opened my eyes. I still had my clothes on from yesterday and the odd smell of the cover over me made me sit up quickly, throwing it off of me. My toes were stiff inside my shoes, as I wiggled them. I hated sleeping with my shoes on, ugh! I could hear voices chatting as I rose from the couch heading to the bathroom. I walked slowly past Nanny's cracked room door hoping I could hear what they were talking about. No one noticed me creeping past Nanny's room door as they chatted about the previous night's events. I eased into the bathroom, using only enough force to catch the latch as I closed the bathroom door. I quickly used the restroom so I wouldn't miss any part of the muffled conversation. Taking a couple steps out of the bathroom I stood still in the shadows of the dimmed hallway, quiet barely breathing.

"That girl got herself into some damn trouble. I told Patsy that nigga wasn't no good! I have Janee here with me, Willie dropped her off last night.", Nanny said in an irritated tone. I wondered who she was talking to because I could only see the dark coat of a male figure sitting opposite of her bed when I snuck past. "Petey came in tripping and she tried to get dressed and go out to the Collins Club. She put on a dress and he ripped it off of her. She went and put on another damn dress and he hit her and ripped that one off too! Then she put on another dress and tried to rip that one off and she gutted his big ass! You know Patsy doesn't play about her clothes and she was drinking too. That Indian blood took over and she almost killed his ass, cutting him down the center of his stomach!", she said laughing. "Only thing is, now she has landed herself in trouble and in jail. These white people are not playing with black folks!"

In jail I thought? What the hell? Is that why she never came outside? Is that why her ex boyfriend picked me up? I started to cry. Tears flowed down my face and I started to think what am I going to do without my mother? My summer was ruined and I waited so patiently to come and spend the summer with my mother in her new apartment. My presence was detected and I wasn't sure if I was crying too loud or if it was due to Nanny knowing every movement that takes place in her house. Nonetheless she gestured for me to come into her room.

I trudged down the hall dragging my feet, every step feeling as heavy as the one before it. Cigarette and weed smoke filled my nose upon entering her room. Being cautious of the overwhelming contents of her room I tried to watch my step through my watery eyes. Nanny motioned for me to come closer and as I got closer she grabbed me and hugged me tight. I cried and cried, losing track of time on how long she was embracing me. I melted in her huge fluffy arms and she began to rock back and forth. She whispered, "Your dad called for you to check on you. He told me to take you to your Grandma's. house for the rest of the summer. You can stay with us if you want." Shaking my head no, I just wanted to get away from any place that would remind me of her. Staying here would only make me want and miss her more. Nanny shifted my body so I could look her directly into her eyes and said, "If you need me or want to come here just ask, ok." Hitting me on my butt to dismiss me she handed me a cigarette and told me to go light her cigarette. "Somebody is always stealing my damn lighters!" she yelled sternly.

CHAPTER 13

Our personalities are sometimes shaped inadvertently from how we are genetically designed. I was a good kid that loved structure, loved cooking, and felt domesticated at a young age. My youthfulness never hindered my passion or built in desire to help people or make myself available to others. My grandmother was the same way, just an older version. The time spent with my father's mother was often limited due to my constant travels. Yet I was identical to someone I rarely spent time with.

My mom going to jail changed that quickly and I was now expected to spend the Summer with my overly perfect grandmother. Everything was perfect! Her neatly rowed backyard garden, the plastic guarded living room furniture, spotless kitchen, organized laundry room, meticulous sewing room, the bottles of perfume on her huge vanity dresser, the tucks and corners of every bed in the home, and even her tightly curled jet black Creole hair.

I stood patiently in front of the iron gate separating the walkway from the front door, by about eight feet. Anticipation filled my body, thinking about how tight her hugs usually are, and how she would practically leave my cheek wet after greeting me. There's something about a tight hug that I despise. Being bonded tightly and not being able to move frightens the hell out of me. So I shifted my weight from side to side waiting for her to answer the door.

Her chuckle filled my ears as the door swung open. She smiled every step of the way, sounding as jolly as Santa Claus when she laughed. Her gold tooth glistened in the morning sun and the many wind chimes on the porch swayed making theme music for her entrance. I stood still trying to hold onto my raggedy suitcase awaiting the next journey that awaited. My visits to her house in the past were short. Two and a half months was going to seem like forever here!

"Look at you Nae-Nae!", she said, smothering me with an attack of kisses all over my face, and squeezing me tightly. I tried really hard not to be rude and pull back and just let her work her magic.

"I'm glad you've come to stay with me and Papoo! Sorry to hear about your mom. That Patsy." she said, shaking her head. I could tell she was asking herself "What has Patsy gotten herself into?" Nana didn't express it verbally and she didn't have to, everyone was thinking the same thing.

I followed Nana into her fortress of perfection. My eyes never even glanced toward the forbidden living room, and my feet made squeaking noises as we walked down the foyer over one of many plastic runners that existed in her home. We made a left into the short hallway making another left into her sewing room. I hated that room because it reeked of moth balls. I slid my suitcase under the bed and shook my head in assurance of her wishes of not touching her sewing machine.

Despite the time frame of visits to her house, I already knew my next stop was the restroom to freshen up. Everything was the same. The fan hummed in the background when I flicked on the bathroom light, compensating for the missing window in the architecture. The floors were covered with fresh fluffy bathroom rugs. Spotless was an understatement, because she cleaned it everyday. I turned on the sink and grabbed the shell shaped soap next to the nozzles and washed my hands, staring at the chicken pox scar under my right eye on my cheek bone. "Ugh", I thought. "Still ugly!" as I flicked off the light as I exited the bathroom.

***

About six weeks passed and I was withering into a ball of boredom. My grandmother and grandfather's strict daily routine was deeply embedded into me and I could follow their program blindly.

ETERNAL BAGGAGE

Somedays I would try to lie in bed until she made me get up, just to have less time in the day to be awake.

Mornings always began early around 7am or 8am. Coffee filled the air and I could hear the percolating coffee pot on the stove. My grandmother's fresh homemade biscuits sat in the middle of the kitchen table on a special saucer designed with flowers. I would eat Quaker oatmeal and she was so great at preparing it that I would try to retrieve every kernel of oats inside the bowl with my spoon.

After I got dressed, I would wander around the house while she worked in the garden or was ironing in her washroom. The tv was usually on the Price is Right and I would enjoy sitting in my grandpa's leather recliner while I watched. No one was allowed in his chair if he was at home! His absence from home gave me endless opportunities to take advantage of flopping around in his chair as if it belonged to me. When the gardening was done my grandmother and I would run errands in her red Toyota Camry. My mind would drift off and I would imagine myself knowing how to drive, driving her car. I silently pulled my hair out as she took her time cruising the streets to the grocery store and making her routine stop at the bank.

Although the mornings and days were extremely boring, I dreaded the evenings. I think because bedtime was around 8 o'clock and to a young kid that's torcher especially due to the fact it was the Summertime! I had no understanding of why we were going to bed early to get up early and to do the exact same shit we did yesterday. The evenings were preparation for another tomorrow. It was an endless lap around the track of life, in Nana's world.

Dinner was the best part of the evening, my grandmother was the best cook ever. Her food always melted in my mouth and the anticipation of eating left me waiting impatiently eyeballing her every move in the kitchen. One thing I couldn't put my finger on was when did she cook?

Most nights she went to her freezer and pulled out tupperware dishes and microwaved leftovers.

Each time it tasted like a meal freshly prepared on the spot. I hope to cook as good as her when I grow up and figured I would eventually learn because my dad was a great cook like her too!

Dinner was amazing and I would have licked the bowl if my grandmother would allow it. The bowl of cioppino didn't last very long after my grandpa blessed the food and we began eating. I loved the American-Italian dish! The blend of all the seafood and red sauce over a bed of rice was quite delectable. The comfort of food made me forget how much I despise evenings here. I ran my bath water and hurried to jump in the water, the spontaneity of Nana bursting in the door was at an all time high. She always creeped me out when she came in to bring fresh towels or soap, so I moved quickly not taking any chances.

I relaxed in the tub and thought about my mother. Everyday I was here I wrote to my mother. It was easy to gather writing materials. There was a desk in the sewing room where I slept. A yellow college ruled notepad with notes written on it was on the desk and a box of small and large envelopes sat side by side next to a cup that held several pens and pencils. I would write to my mom and tell her how much I loved and missed her. I always ended the letter expressing I couldn't wait to go live with her when she got out of the drug program. I loved my mother and no matter what place or who I was pawned off too, being in her presence was mandatory in my spirit.

I grabbed all my dirty clothes after making sure the bathroom was spotless and the tub was cleaned before exiting the bathroom. When I opened the door my grandmother waited on the other side of the door, eyes burning with fury. I didn't know what I did but apparently it wasn't good.

"Come in here girl!", she yelled, gesturing for me to follow her. When I entered her sewing room and what was known to me as the guest room I saw all her beautiful church dresses laying on the bed. I looked at them spread on the bed. I was confused about what was happening and why she was so angry.

"Why'd you cut up my clothes, little girl?" she demanded to know. I stared at her with a disconcerting look on my face, not knowing what to say next.

Beginning with the truth I began, "I didn't cut your dresses Nana" holding my head down. Afraid of what would happen to me, I stated "I promise I didn't cut your clothes."

"I don't believe you! What would make you do something like that?" Tears trickled down my cheeks as I fought to hold my tears back.

"You won't be staying in my house. I don't deal with liars or nonsense like that!", she yelled. She didn't believe me. I was afraid my dad was going to be pissed once he found out. I'm sure he would take her side and I would probably get a whooping for it once he saw me face to face.

Nana left the room ranting on and on, "I know she did it, ain't nobody been in that room in months!" I felt terrible and knew my stay would come to an end soon. Even though I was bored out of my mind I enjoyed her warm hospitality and learning things from her and Papoo. The truth didn't matter and I had no idea of how I could possibly persuade her into believing I was being honest.

I solemnly layed down after putting all my things into my raggedy tan suitcase. Remembering I received a letter from my mother I grabbed it off the desk and began reading it:

Dear Nae-Nae,

How are you doing? Good I hope. I'm sure Nana is treating you well, her and Papoo. They are such good people. Nana and Papoo always treated me like their daughter even though your dad and I got a divorce and he remarried. Thank you for the letters you have been writing to me. It feels good to get them from you. They always make my day. I'm sorry you even have to write to me in this God forsaken place. I will be moving to an alcohol and drug program soon then you can come see me. Take care and be good! Love you Nae-Nae and I can't wait to get another letter from you.

Love, Mommy

I folded the letter back up, remembering to place it back in the envelope it came in. I walked over to the closet to put it with the rest of my things in my raggedy suitcase. When I pulled my suitcase out of the closet a box came out with it. Staring puzzled at the box, the dim light hid what was written on the small empty box. Picking up the small box, I walked it over to the lamp on the wooden desk to get a better look. The box read: Enoz Old Fashioned Moth Balls! No way I thought. I walked to the closet and through it back in the closet and sat my suitcase by the foot of the bed near the cracked room door. The empty mothball box explains why her clothes had holes in them. I shook my head with the satisfaction of knowing I truly was telling the truth as I climbed into bed. Smiling to myself I pulled the covers up to my neck and drifted peacefully to sleep.

CHAPTER 14

The first time I fell in love was when I laid eyes on my 8 pounds 4 ounces bundle of joy. I never wanted children. If I was going to play the part of being straight, giving birth to a child was inevitable. I mean I was already settling for having a boyfriend and our relationship in my eyes was mediocre. Everyone knew we were an item. Outside of our relationship, they also knew Cory was a two-timing cheater! I truly felt in a sense we were both using one another and it was working in our favor. He lived with his father and all his older brothers, so all he knew was dog females. He got to pretend he actually wanted a monogamous relationship and I got to pretend I actually enjoyed being with a guy. Ugh!

My son's eyes were big and brown and stared back at me as if we've known each other forever. I held him close to my chest wrapped inside the hideous white, pink, and light blue hospital blankets. I admired the neat foldings of the blanket because it made holding him easier. The anticipation of difficulty holding him did not bother me once I held him for the first time. His abnormally huge size made it easier. Cory J'ray Lewis was born at 8 pounds 4 ounces. I will never forget how his hair was curly and tickled my nose the 1st time I kissed him on the top of his head. His brown round eyes glistened as I stared into them and I got lost in them feeling transparent. I felt a genuine bond that no one or nothing could ever break.

Lil' Man grew so fast right before my eyes. He was one years old before I knew it. His stocky body frame and invisible neckline reminded me of a Lil' Man, so that's what adopted the nickname Lil' Man. He was so funny and loving. I loved teaching him how to do things like feed or dress himself. He was a human sponge and learned so much at a faster rate than other children his age. Lil' Man would sing along to any song he heard, and was quite comical when he sung songs he didn't know the words too. We spent a lot of time outside and his ability to mimic gross motor movements was mind blowing. By the time he reached two and half years old he could ride a two wheeled bike! Lil' Man was riding his first bike, balancing on two wheels. He was unaware that the training wheels had not been touching the ground for support, for weeks. I felt so proud the day I took the pliers and removed them from his back tire! The speed he would travel through our bungalow style apartment complex was astonishing.

***

    The lord blessed me with a one bedroom apartment by the time he turned 2 years old. I was so excited to decorate his room. His white metal bunk bed was covered with spiderman linen and filled with all his toys. I bought a futon style couch for the living room so I could have a place to sleep. I wanted the bedroom to only be for him. My sacrifice as a mother was to wait patiently for a bigger living space that would provide two bedrooms. Until then I maintain my composure and slept in the living room. I didn't mind it very much. I decorated the living room so nicely with pictures and trinkets. When people visited they wouldn't even have guessed I slept in the living room.

    Lil' Man became my world and living on our own now provided even more time for us to bond. His father loved the idea of us living in an apartment away from my parents house on Ralmar Street. The distance gave him time to slither around with other females. I didn't care at the least. I was proud of my independence and free of the dark shadow, my unbearable step sister. Cory would visit Lil' Man all the time and sometimes spent the night with him in his room. He always bought him video games which may sound peculiar. Age was not a factor, only being 3 he was a video game prodigy! His skills left me feeling very low some days as if I was playing the video game creator.

Lil' Man was learning so much! I taught him to make instant oatmeal, how to ride a skateboard, how to write his homework perfectly with astounding penmanship! I couldn't have been more proud of his accomplishments. I began making friends with some of the neighboring tenants in my apartment complex. The females I met were a tad bit rowdy and urban, but very good friends. Who was I to judge? I enjoyed their company and they definitely distracted me from the bullshit relationship I was in.

On Lil' Man's 4th Birthday, I received confirmation that my so-called relationship with his father had come to an end. I expected him to visit Lil' Man for his birthday and to make an appearance at his party but he never showed up. We had an amazing time despite his father's absence. My cousins and I decorated our tiny apartment with Pokémon decorations. My mother got him a cake with Pokémon decorations on one side and a picture of Lil' Man on the other half of the cake. A lot of children attended. We played games, ate good food, danced, and sang Happy Birthday with a cake fight to end the festivities. My son was happy so I didnt even worry that Cory never showed his sneaky, black ass, that day.

The kitchen was the last thing I cleaned after the party. I reflected on how many children I crammed into our tiny apartment for Lil' Man's birthday party. Shaking my head in dismay I basked in the moment. Despite our small venue selection, Lil' Man's birthday was a hit.

Laying on the small futon in the living room also known as my bedroom by night, my eyes began to feel heavy. The small apartment provided great comfort for me from the outside world and I held my pillow tight, drifting off to sleep. The loud bangs on the door interrupted my peaceful sleep, and I would have thought I was dreaming if it hadn't been followed by the yelling of, "Open up, Menlo Park Police Department!" No way I thought to myself stumbling to the front door a couple of feet away from the squeaky futon.

Peering through the small peep hole, I could see about seven uniformed cops waiting outside the door. I opened the door and stood back as they bum rushed me, pushing me aside to enter the apartment.

"Good evening Mam, we were alerted that Cory Lewis resides at this residence."

Counteracting their assumptions, "No he doesn't live here, only my son and I live here. Cory comes to visit and spends the night sometimes, but he doesn't live here!"

"Well he says he lives here and gave this address as his place of residence. We have to search the premises because he is on probation and was just arrested on drug charges, giving us probable cause to search this apartment. Can you have a seat? Is there anyone else in the unit?"

Shaking my head, yes. I sat down, "just my son officer, he's asleep."

The officers began to spread out searching the bathroom, the living room, and going through cabinets in the kitchen. The tiny Section 8 apartment reached its maximum occupancy, as the men in blue scattered into different areas in search of paraphernalia. Between the police occupying more space than allotted, I shivered indiscreetly. I sucked in all the air in the apartment and held my breath as they searched the bedroom. They brought Lil' Man into the living room half asleep and made him sit next to me on the futon. He looked confused and I could tell he was terribly afraid. I kept leaning forward looking into the bedroom afraid of what they might find. Remembering back a few nights, Cory came to visit Lil' Man and toted a huge backpack with him containing god knows what. In no way shape or form was I ready to serve time or be an accomplice to what was in the backpack if it was still here.

I could hear compliments of how tidy and clean the apartment was and they all gathered back in the living room apologizing for the inconvenience. One by one they exited out the front door. My heart raced during the entire probation search and began to slow down as I watched them one by one leave through the front door. Lost in thought my mind wandered as I dreaded the alternative impact of how things would have ended. I held my chest with relief; pondering their lack of knowledge concerning the backpack with its mysterious content buried in its hiding spot. The closet was hidden by the open room door. With the open room door they couldn't see that the wall

ETERNAL BAGGAGE

directly behind the room door stood a closet door of doom. Thank you lord! Never in a million years did I think the small layout of this apartment would literally save my life! My deep thoughts were broken by the last cop exiting the apartment, "You know Cory is going to jail for a long time? He had an ounce of crack cocaine in the car with him and the other young lady." Smiling, he pulled the door shut.

The other young lady, I thought? That motherfucker! So he was out cheating! And during his son's party? "That's what he gets!", I yelled aloud. "God don't like ugly!" Disgusted with finding out the reason Cory missed Lil' Man's party I completely forgot about the backpack. I tucked Lil' Man back into bed and went around the house putting everything back in its place, closing drawers and cabinets along the way. I definitely acquired the cleaning while your mad trait that most women adhibit, because I finished putting everything back in its place in record time. I plopped onto the soft but stiff futon mistaking it for a real couch and hurt my tailbone in the process. "Ouch!", I yelled aloud, forgetting not to wake Lil Man. I sat in silence for a spell, still in awe that the police didn't find what they were looking for and that I still had my freedom. "Wait a minute!" I thought to myself as I jumped up running quietly to the dark bedroom.

I opened the closet without making any noise, careful not to wake Lil' Man. Bending down in the dark space I retrieved the backpack, from the "hidden" closet. Closing the room door behind me, I turned on the lamp, straining my fingers to twist the skinny metal switch on the neck of the lamp. "Cheap ass Walmart lamp!", I thought to myself. I unzipped the zipper belonging to the larger compartment to the backpack. I was as careful as a terrorist with a homemade bomb.

Inside were two large ziplock bags with smaller bags in each one. I counted them out as I took each one out one by one. The first one had sixteen and the second one had eight. I had never seen so much weed in my life! I mean, not at one time for that matter. I had seen it on television but not in real life and not in my own possession. Unzipping the other small compartments, I found two more small sandwich baggies. One had a huge white powdery rock in it and the other had a bunch of minuscule plastic wrapped rocks inside. "Spitters" is what all the street boys called it.

They bagged them up like that so they could swallow them if the police tried to arrest them. I was naive at times, but living in my neighborhood I was exposed to many things.

My lack of knowledge on drug dealing didn't hinder me from making money. I asked around on my trips to the corner store, across the Willow Road and Bay Road intersection. Everyday for about two weeks I asked the guys hanging out questions about "tree" and the prices. I needed to know as much as possible, if I was going to sell what I had and profit off of it. I was careful when I inquired around leaving out details about the package I had acquired. My detective days were short lived when I stumbled across someone who needed almost everything I had. No way in hell was I going to risk being robbed. Asking the wrong person which could possibly lead to just that!

I dumped everything I had in less than a week to a couple of guys from my neighborhood. One was an O.G. also known as Original Gangster and a younger gentleman familiar from my high school days. After Lil' Man was bathed and in bed. I broke down a Swisher sweet into my spotless garbage can. I smiled to myself, proud of how my keen eye for detail gave me the ability to keep it clean. I took the last small ziploc baggie out of my secret stash and began crumbling some of the Nuggets I laid on the kitchen table. Next I sprinkled the small pile of greenery on the swisher, dusting my hands on my basketball shorts. Without even thinking I tucked in one side of the cigarillo as if I was making a bed in the military. I was careful not to do it too tight. I didn't want to split the blunt. I think I moved so quickly because I was anxious about counting the money I made. I licked the open side of the swisher and closed it with ease in one swipe.

I went outside and sat on the short wooden frame outside my tiny apartment door. Carefully I cuffed one hand to block the wind as I lit my blunt at the larger end of my perfectly rolled masterpiece. I inhaled the strong aroma of White Widow Kush. I learned the specifics of the strand I was trying to move and how potent it was during my adventure in selling it. Admitting to myself when I coughed that it was definitely living up to its reputation of being a top shelf strand. After a few pulls of the blunt I went back into the house and I pulled the money I made out of the inside hidden pocket of the backpack. Carefully I organized the bills in sequence in stacks of 100's, 50's, 20's,10's and so on. Beginning with the hundred dollar bills I counted them licking the tips of my fingers to prevent any bills from sticking together. I never had this much money at one time in my entire life! I recounted the money several times losing count when I got close to almost $8,000. I finally gave up and put it in a huge stack, getting nervous about having so much cash. I took everything 20 and over and put it in a sock and hid it at the back of my hidden closet. Feeling safe once it was safely put up I took the other bills and put it in my pants pocket of the clothes I was wearing the next day. I couldn't believe the money I made. For once I felt secure and not stressed. I wasn't even worried about Cory being mad about his stuff or even getting any of the profits. "Serves him right!", I whispered. It felt good. I was starting to like revenge! And yes it felt great, it felt pretty damn awesome!

CHAPTER 15

Sometimes without being aware we subconsciously act out revenge against someone we momentarily despise, feel anger towards, or have harmed us in some form. Most of the time it's the universe's way of coming full circle returning the energy good or bad that one has released. Nonetheless, as humans we connect past feelings with current emotions, and allow our past to dictate how we act in the now. Sometimes in events of karma our lack of empathy or guilt schemes us into thinking we are getting revenge, when merely we are allowing the universe to work its magic.

Magic. Who believes in magic? Besides the quick hand tricks one has seen in a setting such as Fisherman's Wharf or Market Street in San Francisco or at a famous show at the Mandalay in Las Vegas. My first time seeing good karma also known as magic, came to life right before my eyes. I found it hard to believe that it was actually happening as I watched the many 20, 50, and 100 dollar bills fall from the sky.

***

I counted out some change from my piggy bank, which actually was a large mason jar. I skimmed through the coins and I only selected the silver coins. I scraped together enough to put together with the 8 dollar bills I had, to get gas, a short pack of Newport Menthol Cigarettes, and Swisher Sweet cigar.

I backed out of my parking stall into the alley located behind my quaint single story apartment building. I prayed out loud begging God to make it possible for me to make it to the gas station, without running out of gas. The sun struck my face and my arm, almost melting my skin even behind the tinted windows of my GMC Jimmy Diamond Edition truck. I wish I had enough money to go somewhere. I weaved in between and around cars that took too long to turn or even drive straight. Every so often I glanced at the red "Low Fuel" light, blinking on the dashboard. Finally I pulled into the Chevron gas station with relief. Tripping over my own feet, I hurried inside to pay for my gas and other items. I was trying to move quickly while the inside was empty, so no one would see me counting so much change. I couldn't bear the embarrassment on top of my self pity of being broke. "Ugh", I thought to myself. I hated being broke.

    I climbed back into my truck as I split the Swisher flawlessly down the middle. Removing the air vent, I reached into the secret hiding spot for my tree. I had just enough to roll up a Swisher. I glanced around checking my surroundings as I blindly broke down the tree into the Swisher. I gathered all the tiny nugs that ended up in my lap and plopped them into the gutted cigar.

    Carefully I licked and rolled the blunt without even looking at it. Frantically I patted my pockets as I scoped around the car for my lighter. My cell phone rang and it was my friend Tania. "Ay Nae, whatcha doing?", she asked. "Where are you at blood? Pull up I know you have some tree." "Aight!", I said, throwing the phone onto the passenger seat as I ended the call.

    I eagerly drove to Tania's house so I could finish my attempt to smoke my last blunt. I rapidly turned the car off, and I grabbed the blunt from the ashtray. My OCD made me look back at the car at least 2 or 3 times, when I locked the car door as the alarm blared loudly.. I jogged up to the door and walked in without knocking. I nodded at Tania's father as I walked towards her room door. Surprised it was open, I pushed the door open even more as I entered. Exaggerating I yelled, "What's up nigga!" and flopped down on her bed. Clearing a space for me to be comfortable I threw the pile of clothes to the side onto a clothes basket.

    "Fire that blunt up, I haven't smoked all day!", Tania dramatized.

"I just barely smoked myself," I replied as I passed her the blunt. "Man it's boring as fuck! I hate being broke because it makes it even more boring."

After inhaling the blunt she blew out the smoke saying,"You ain't never lied!"

"I was wishing I had money Ness so we could at least slide to Great America!" We made small talk while we smoked. We did our best to enjoy the only blunt we would smoke, until we came up with some money.

The door swung open as I attempted to put the doobie out in the ashtray filled with Newport cigarette butts. I jumped, dropping the lit doobie onto the floor. Irritated with being frightened, I grabbed the roach before it burned the carpet and tossed it into the ashtray. "What the hell yall doing in here?" said Tania's little sister, Chelsea. Giggling with her friend Nesha, the two of them sat on their knees at the edge of the bed. "It's so boring. We should go to Great America!", Chelsea said as she adjusted her bra strap so it wouldn't show from under her tank top strap. "We're broke!" Tania and I yelled in unison and broke out in laughter. "I dont see what's so funny?", Chelsea said angrily. "Yall must be high."

"Well if we had money, we wouldn't be sitting here dummy!", Tania said.

We sat in silence for what seemed like forever. I began to hear white noise as we sat quietly. I could hear the clock ticking in her living room, my heart beating, and the faint dripping sound of water from her bathroom faucet up the hall. Nesha's whispering voice broke the silence, "I know where we can get some money. My grandma has money. She won't even notice if I take some. I can get enough for us all to go to Great America."

"Oh, hell nah!" Tania and I spoke again in unison.

"You are not taking money from your Grandma! Forget about it!" Tania firmly disputed.

"It's my money anyway. She doesn't ever give me money. I barely go anywhere. My grandma doesn't buy me clothes and she gets a check for me! I can't even get my hair done. Look at my hair.

I don't care if I'm getting money today. Are you guys going to give me a ride?"

We looked at each other, and telepathically agreed. Tania and I stood up, "I'll drive!" I said.

I thought to myself this is wrong on so many levels. My first thought weighed the first. I thought about how all the kids would tease Nesha for being less attractive. They would talk about her acne, her hair style, her outdated clothes, and how she could never leave the house. "Fuck it", I instantly came to a conclusion thinking about her misfortunes. She deserves some money and to go somewhere, at the very least. Nesha reassured us she wouldn't get caught or snitch if she did. She agreed to only get money for us all to go to Great America and to put gas in the tank. I figured what harm would she cause? My mouth was saying one thing, my gut gave me another feeling.

We sat in the truck going over possible scenarios, and paranoia set in with us all. The various scenarios we conjured up with our cauldron full of guilt were now boiling over. What if she gets caught? Will her grandma notice the money is missing? Will Nesha be put on punishment? What if she calls the police? Will we all get in trouble with the law? Nesha never gave in and she was so determined to do what she came to her house to do. Nesha's aggressive body language made me believe she was fed up. She slammed her fist on her knees and groaned in frustration.

A voice of reason spoke up, "Shut the fuck up blood! We've been sitting here debating if she should take the money or not? It's Nesha's idea so we have nothing to worry about. Nesha's grandma was playing her anyway, keeping all her money. She doesn't get her hair braided, doesn't buy her clothes and shit. Nesha I know you are tired of living the real life Cinderella story! Nesha, if you are about to go in there and get the money, then we're gonna have fun!" Tania shook her head aggravated with our negative thoughts on the situation.

Without notice Nesha hopped out the rear seat of my truck and walked up to her house. Nesha's grandma's car was not in the driveway so the "coast was clear" I thought, as I lit a cigarette.

Tania and I passed it back and forth, never taking our eyes off the house. Chelsea looked back every time she heard an approaching car and watched the street. Chelsea never missed a car as they traveled up and down the block. "I hope her grandma doesn't come," she said nervously.

Twenty minutes passed and Nesha still had not come out of the house. We all were worried now. "Maybe her grandma is in the house but her car just isn't here.", Chelsea continued.

"Blood shut up!", demanded Tania.

"There she is! She's running out. What is that she's carrying?" questioned Chelsea. I turned the ignition and Tania reached behind her and swung the door open. Nesha threw her body in and almost ended up in Chelsea's lap. I could smell the mixture of Prostyle gel, sweat, and desperation as she moved around in the back seat. Her body flung again towards Chelsea as I made a sharp right turn onto Clark Street, and headed back to the Gardens. The Gardens also known as G-town is a neighborhood with streets named after flowers. It's also the area where each generation becomes an heir to their parent's stature or power in the street games. Also they are blessed with connections and money.

Nesha and Chelsea cheered loudly in the backseat chanting, "We're going to Great America, we're going to Great America!"

"Ok, ok, ok with the cheerleading and shit. Where's the money you were supposed to get? All you came out with is a silver box." Tania stated the obvious.

"This is the money. Well, I mean it's inside this box. I was looking everywhere for the key but I couldn't find it."

"So how are we going to get the money and put the box back Nesha? Are you trying to get caught?" Tania cleaned her nails with a torn matchbook cover, while she waited for an answer. "We cannot open that box without breaking it, so we have to put it back, genius! Nae turn around rogue, so she can put that box back."

"No! We are keeping it and I will just deny it if she asks if I took it. I wanna go to Great America!"

"Alright Nesha, it better not be any shit about this box. And you better not snitch blood! Nae go to the house so we can open this box. Nesha draped a jacket over the box to hide it from Tania and Chelsea's dad as we suspiciously entered the house. Tania veered from the pack of thieves and headed towards the garage. Smart idea, I thought. We are going to need tools to open that box. Tania closed her room door behind her and threw the tools on the bed when she returned from the garage. They made a loud clanking noise on impact to the mattress.

Nesha pulled the jacket from around the silver box. The box flipped a couple times inches above the mattress and landed on the center of the bed. Tania, Chelsea, Nesha and I stared at each other. Our eyes said to each other "Are we sure we want to do this?" Nesha anxiously grabbed the box and shook it knowing it wouldn't open without the key.

"Blood, are you sure you want to break it open? Once we open it ain't no turning back." Tania twirled the hammer and screwdriver, one in each hand. Her eyebrows raised for confirmation from Nesha to proceed.

"Bust that shit open!" Nesha said with authority.

Tania wedged the tip of the flat head screwdriver she held, into the space between the lid and the base of the metal box. She struck the handle of the screwdriver with the hammer, careful enough to avoid her hand on contact. Nothing happened, just a loud clanking sound. Tania paused and looked towards the closed room door to listen out for her father. She reached back a little more than the first time, displaying she would increase more force in her swing. Her right hand came down and nicked her left hand that held the screwdriver steadily. She dropped both tools on the bed, "Goddammit!" she yelled. We all watched in suspense, ready for her to try again. Picking up the tools she did two practice swings, coming close to the handle of the screwdriver. Her arm went back for a third time and struck the screwdriver down into the metal box. Nesha grabbed the box and pulled backwards on the screwdriver, bending the lid of the box backwards. A small crack revealed the contents of the box, which was a lot of money. Overwhelmed with the sudden urge to retrieve the treasure, Nesha began welding on the box with the hammer. Nesha picked up the box and stuck both hands in the open space and pulled her hands apart from one another with the strength of a WCW Wrestler. The box broke open and flew into the air. We all screamed simultaneously when we saw the 20s, 50s, and 100 dollar bills falling onto us, like leaves blowing in an autumn breeze.

Our screams fainted abruptly when we heard a knock at the door. Lamont, Tania's father, spoke with great authority through the closed door.

"What are guys doing in there? What's with all the screaming?"
"Nothing! Sorry!", we said in unison.

We all did the quiet sign with our index finger up to our lips, shushing each other. Still snickering and giggling we scooped all the money into the center of the bed with our arms. Some bills had fallen onto the floor and we added them to the mound as well. Tania and I 1st separated the bills into stacks of 100. Our eyes bulged at the many stacks on the bed. Making room on the bed we awaited on our knees positioned around the bed, the stacks of cash took up more room than we expected.

One of my knees felt uncomfortable and I glanced down to see what was causing the poking sensation in my knee cap. A bulky white envelope with the outside imprint of a rectangular shape was under my leg. Leaving the envelope in its place beside the bed I stared at Tania until she looked back at me. I moved my eyes towards the floor without moving my head and her eyes followed. She smiled at me and gave me a reassuring nod. I pushed the envelope under some clothes on the floor. The stacks of 100 were then divided evenly into groups of four.

Anticipation filled the air as the last stacks were separated. In front of each of us was 25 stacks of a 100 each. "$2500 dollars!", we whispered. We smiled and scooped up our stacks into our hands. We gleamed at how great it felt to hold it. Just less than an hour ago we were broke. Tania laid down some ground rules that she would disperse Nesha's and Chelsea's cash to them when needed. If either of the two went shopping, all items would be left in her room to avoid unwanted attention. Tania said it's better we don't arouse suspicion so Nesha wouldn't get in trouble with her Grandma. Tania gave Chelsea and Nesha 2 100 dollar bills and told them to go start the truck and wait in the car while she stashed the cash in her room.

Tania closed the door tightly as they walked out. "Blood, where is that envelope?", she said.

I pulled it out from under a dirty pair of jeans on the floor where I was sitting and through it on the bed. We smiled as she ripped the envelope open quickly. The contents of the envelope were all 100 dollar bills! We tickled eachother while laughing hysterically. We hurried gained our composure before anyone tried to knock on the door for entry. Holding the big stack in one hand she placed bills down one at a time into two piles. One pile for her and one pile for me. She moved like a professional banker, as she thumbed through the bills as fast as a counting machine. Tania handed me my stack of 100s equaling $5,000 and added her new pile to the previous

$2500 and stashed her money away. Tania and I had $7500 a piece and Nesha and Chelsea had

$2500 each. That means it was a total of $20,000 that Nesha took from her grandmother!

On our fast paced walk to the car Tania whispered, "I hope her ass doesn't tell blood! Nobody is trying to go down for this shit!"

I nodded with approval and walked to my trunk. I grabbed the handle and lifted the heavy door upwards. What started out as a dull day, had started to pick up. The combination of the hot sun and the heat coming from the exhaust pipe made my body start to overheat. I stood behind my truck and hid the stolen cash inside the compartment that hides the car jack and emergency kit. I placed the lid back into the grooves and flipped the latch back into place. I hopped in the Black Diamond Edition GMC Jimmy my father had bought me and cranked the A/C onto the maximum setting.

"So what now?" I said as I pulled from the curb heading to the gas station.

"Shit its only two something. Should we be headed to Great America? It's time to have some fun!", Tania said. "They don't close until 10 tonight so we have plenty of time to have fun!"

It was as if our minds were on the same wavelength because we all yelled, "Thank you Nesha!", and broke out hysterically into non stop laughter.

The next couple of weeks was a complete blur of cash, paranoia, shame, guilt, impulse shopping, and overwhelming mysteries of what was in store for us. The unexpected and well deserved cash flow didn't suffice for the turmoil I seemed to be experiencing. I don't know about anyone else, but I was not feeling very happy about being part of an unknown heist. My brain could not handle what I imagined countless times. I feared the trouble that was in store if we got caught.

My guilt still did not stop me from filling my closet with shoes and clothes for my son and I. I paid some bills and even stocked the refrigerator and cabinets with plenty of food. It felt great to buy whatever I wanted. I despised the fact that I lacked the mental compatibility every now and then to enjoy it.

As the money slowly faded from my various hiding spots, so did Nesha. Her attendance of hanging out with us went from tardy sometimes to complete truancy. None of us spoke of her absence not until the day Chelsea burst into the house with incredible news.

"I saw Nesha yall!" she spoke loudly, interrupting our smoking session for two. We stared at her waiting for her to continue.

"Of course she looked like crap, she always does. Anyway, do you know she has been on punishment since the last time we saw her? She said her grandma was pissed and didn't believe that she did not take the money. Nesha was forced to take a lie detector test at the police station! And guess what? She passed it, she actually passed a lie detector test! Aren't trained spies the only people who can beat a lie detector test. Can you believe it?" Chelsea's voice began to fade after hearing the words that meant we were in the clear.

Tania looked at me with relief, blowing out a dark cloud of smoke as she handed me the blunt. Watching the huge cloud of smoke fill the air after hearing the great news instantly washed away the guilt I felt all these months. Today felt great. Finally I could put my guilt I have been carrying for the past couple months in my emotional suitcase.

CHAPTER 16

The silver lining of a dark cloud often awaits us, if we can get past the darkness we experience. I believe if we focus more on the negative aspects of our everyday life that we are creating our ora to be just that. That theory is easier said than done. I am also guilty of being a negative Nancy. With much practice I eventually retrained my way of thinking. I could find the smallest peace of hope in any situation. Thinking positive, shaped me into an optimistic person. When doubt surfaced, I was indeed prone to utilizing my mistakes as learning lessons. I learn to recreate what I expected my future to be despite its many challenges.

An unfortunate event of a gun going off in Eli's apartment in Long Beach, led to an unexpected call for permission to come live with me. The beginning of our relationship was a lot of cat and mouse behavior. Our connection stated the obvious; we liked each other, me more than him. The secrecy of our intimacy increased when he would visit the Bay Area. Most of the time I was unsure of why I liked Eli. Being obnoxious was his stronger personality trait. He bluntly spoke his mind and lacked empathy. Most women he encountered argued with him because he was quick to offend their lack of beauty, their choice of clothing, and or anything else he felt to call them on. Yet oddly I adored him. I learned to ignore the rash comments and pretended to be oblivious of the foul taste he left in his audience's mouth. There were other things that attracted me more, than people's opinions of him. Eli was an intelligent psych student at a college in Long Beach. His dominant behavior helped him lead the children he supervised as a camp leader. The fact that he had a car, and was always traveling created this magnetic pull to him. I was attracted more to the mystery of his unknown life more than what I could visually see.

Our relationship evolved quickly after he came to live with my son and I in Menlo Park. During our move from a one bedroom apartment into a two bedroom home in the Gardens is when I discovered I was pregnant. Four weeks after I celebrated my first trimester. My ultrasound revealed I would be having a girl. The name of my daughter was already selected. Mychelle Le'shee Williams was written in my fanciest handwriting posted on the refrigerator for almost a year before even dating my daughter's father. My life was finally feeling complete. I was working as a Teacher's Assistant at my son's Elementary school, I lived in the best area in East Palo Alto, I was in a good relationship, and I was socially popular amongst people in the "in crowd". What more could a woman ask for?

Every pregnancy is different and I was quickly learning everyday this pregnancy was opposite of my pregnancy with Lil Man. I loved my body weight with this pregnancy, thin, with a tiny belly. My waistline was tiny but my appetite was massive. I ate 4 meals a day. My breakfast at home began with 4 toasted peanut butter toast. Usually after getting dressed I would visit my cousin.

Markeisha would cook breakfast for me in exchange for a ride sometime that day or for tree that I would get from my baby's father. Of course while I drove her around on her errands, a restaurant would catch my eye for lunch. Dinners were always amazing because my cousin or one of my many associates would offer to hang out at my house and cook. This pregnancy was filled with plenty of food, friends, and an overwhelming emotion of being cared for.

Being overwhelmed with caring friends helped me recognize characteristics about my baby daddy that I was unaware of. Eli's protective personality never faded but his affection for me disappeared as the days passed. The drinking and the partying increased over time. The way he acted attracted unwanted company I cared less to deal with. Eli grew to be more obnoxious and I hardly knew him anymore. I watched surprisingly as the layers peeled back revealing his true self. The embarrassment of waiting past school dismissal at work in a small town, gave me the mental feeling of having my face rubbed in shit. 80% of the times I was picked up late, he was occupied by 1 or 2 friends. The nonchalant attitude expressed was as if he was doing me a favor of retrieving me from work in my vehicle. His unanticipated change in character happened the day I made that dreadful phone call to pick me up early from work.

"Hello you gotta come get me!" I said screaming and crying simultaneously.

"Something happened to Lil Man! He got hurt at tennis camp and I have to go pick him up. They said he wouldn't ride in the ambulance to the hospital!." The words barely let my lips in between breaths as my asthmatic symptoms began to rise due to the anxiety I was experiencing.

"What? I'm on my way!", as the phone abruptly hung up.

My body seemed to float as I wandered through the school campus. I wandered from the playground into my classroom to retrieve my belongings. The walk from class seemed short as I started walking towards the school entrance, I just wanted to kill time before my ride would arrive. The phone call replayed over and over in my head of the 911 operator calling me shortly before I called Eli to come get me. The pleasant voice hardly coincided with the "unknown caller" flashing across my phone screen.

"Hello, may I speak to Janee?" She said pleasantly.

"Yes this is her, may I ask who's speaking?", I said politely.

"Yes my name is Lucille and I am contacting you to inform you that I am with your son Cory and he has fallen into a manhole.", she said calmly, trying not to alarm me.

Too late! "A manhole? What is that? Where is my son? He's supposed to be at tennis camp, is he still there?" I said frantically.

"Yes mam, he is still here. I wanted to call you because he fell into the manhole but he refused to go in the ambulance and said he wanted to call you. Would you mind saying something to him?" She spoke softly.

"So he can hear me? Cory baby? Mommy is coming to get you ok! I'm on my way ok and everything is going to be alright!" I said fighting back a swarm of emotions.

"Mommy…I'm scared. Please come get me!", Cory said crying out in the most terrifying voice ever.

Everything after hearing his voice seemed unreal. It seemed as if I merely blinked and appeared in Eli's friend's car. The ride to the Stanford campus was all a blur as we bobbed and weaved in between traffic up University to reach the campus. I temporarily forgot I had called my mother who worked in Silicon Valley. I didn't remember until I saw her leap from her car after quickly parking. We pulled up into the parking lot at the same time. My mom, Eli, and I silently power walked down the long walkway. No one spoke a word as we walked towards the location of the large grassy area the 911 dispatcher described. It was when Cory was in my sight that the silence was broken and I began to jog towards him. I completely forgot that I was with child as I glided towards him.

"Oh my God, my baby!"rang through the ears of the campus students and Looky Lous near the small group of people formed around my son.

Lil Man's body was covered in mud and muddy water! I barely recognized the new Gap outfit I dressed him in this morning. The white and navy blue polo shirt and V-neck sweater combo looked like it belonged in a Tide commercial. Lil Man's navy blue cargo shorts were torn in some places and covered in mud too. I hugged him tight as the 911 dispatcher relayed more info than the camp counselors that were supposed to be supervising him. He cried while hugging me back and asked me to not leave him. As I began to examine his body I spotted a huge bump on the back of his head the size of a golf ball. It made me worry because it was protruding out the back of his head. Trying not to show how frantic I was I grabbed his hand and began walking to my mom's car. I completely left the small group of people behind without looking back. I sat in the front passenger seat of my mom's BMW when I reached the car. Every few seconds I looked back and forth over the seat to check on Lil Man during the short ride to the emergency room.

We were only a couple of mins away from the emergency and to me we could not arrive sooner. I begged Eli to watch Lil Man and not allow him to fall asleep. During head injuries the important thing to do is keep the victim awake? After the 3rd or 4th time looking back to check on him he began to slouch lethargically in his seat.

My emotions raced as we got out of the car and rushed into the doors of the Emergency room. My hands trembled as I signed the admin sheet with Lil Man' name. My emotions were weakening me by the second thinking about the golf ball size knot on the back of his head. In my heart I knew something was terribly wrong. I barely made it to sit next to Lil Man before the triage nurse called us to the tiny cubicle to check in. I held onto Lil Man to comfort him, watching his body language closely for any signs that meant he may have sustained head trauma. She went through a series of routine questions asking by his name, age, weight and things of that nature. He sat patiently chiming in with the answers he knew and she began to take his vital signs. The nurse typed rapidly on the keyboard as she quickly entered his information.

Upon finishing his triage intake she motioned for us to return to our seats, reassuring us someone would call us back promptly.

My mom greeted us with a worried look when we returned to our seats. I could tell by how she fidgeted with her purse that it was time for her to take a cigarette break. It wasn't long before we were called to come back into the observation room. I knew things were serious because the nurses informed us that only one adult was allowed to come back to the room. Fighting back my tears of nervousness, I nodded to Eli and my mom to reassure them I would be back soon. In the back of my mind, I was also looking for validation that I could handle what news awaited once we saw a physician. My heart began to race as we entered a large room that looked more like an operating room than a standard room for patients.

Lil Man was sat onto a hospital bed by one of the Emergency Room Nurses. His legs swung back and forth as the nurses began to ask him similar questions that the triage nurse asked. To me he seemed fine. His body language appeared to be normal. He was reserved as any child would be around strange people they don't know. Lil Man and I watched as everyone moved around quickly and he answered the questions as he did before with no problem.

"Hi young man. How are you feeling?" "I'm fine."

"You seemed to have gotten hurt. Do you know how you got hurt?" "Yes I fell in a hole."

"Oh no, well my friends and I are going to take good care of you." "Where were you when you fell?"

"I was at a tennis camp."

"Oh ok, I see.", replied the nurse as she jotted down notes. "Can you tell me how old you are?"

"Yes I'm sith."

Sith, I thought to myself. You mean six, right? You don't talk baby talk and you for sure don't have a lisp. Confused at Lil Man' answer, my eyebrows scrunched together in confusement. "Would you mind telling me what your name is?"

"Yeth, it's Corwee Lewith."

It was at that moment that I knew something was terribly wrong. Tears began to roll down my face as I tried to hide it by quickly wiping my tears with the back of my hand.

The answer to the Nurse's next question sent me into a stage of panic and distress. "Cory, do you know who is standing with you?"

Our eyes met before Cory even answered. Time appeared to have slightly slowed down, because it seemed like forever before he responded.

"No", he said faintly as his mouth drooped to one side and he shrugged his shoulders in an I don't know fashion.

I could no longer fight the tears or my reaction back any longer. I began to question what's wrong and reached out for him but was intervened by another medical staff not to touch him. Everyone moved so fast as they began cutting his clothing off of him. I fought to push past them. I tried to get to him but they forcefully told me I needed to return to the waiting room.

"I'm not leaving my son! I can't leave him while he is like that. He doesn't even know who I am!", I cried out hysterically.

"Mam please come with me", as they directed me out of the large room into the hallway and into a small room with a few chairs in it. Once inside the room I could see the seriousness in the physician's face, when she asked if I would like a phone to call my family.

"Why do I need to call my family?", I questioned sternly.

"Your son is going to have to endure emergency brain surgery. It appears he has sustained a major head trauma. We will first do a CAT scan and following the procedure we will let you know of the damage and what will specifically be done during his operation."

Her words faintly drifted away from my ears, as I began to pray. Silently I murmured "Please Lord, please let my son be ok."

This wasn't actually happening? It couldn't be happening right now I thought. My palms were sweaty and my heart felt heavy. I had never felt so helpless in my life. I was his mother and there was nothing I could do to help him or make him better. The fate of my child's existence was now in the hands of the Stanford Medical Staff. The only one who could fix this was God.

I repeated to him over and over "Please God, please let my son be ok."

CHAPTER 17

The daily familiarity in my life continued to weigh me down. Little by little my thoughts, my emotions, and my soul, lurked the absence of normalcy. Everything pertaining to me was never plain or straightforward. What appeared to be good was not what I expected once the layers revealed its outcome. The phrase, "That's Life!" was overrated and my perspective of how to live life was obstructed. In my mind everything began good, and ended badly. I normally struggled through it, and repeated the never-ending cycle. Relationships, friendships, acquaintances, and even family were difficult to surpass. Over the years optimism became a prominent and vital characteristic of my existence. Constantly I was challenged to see the light in every dark tunnel of my life. Repeatedly at every turn in my path lay a dark shadow to devour me.

Inevitably I acquired "learned habits" due to the misfortunate events I endured. I wanted to love those I felt worthy of love. Naively, I was hurt by everyone. Mostly boys took advantage of my longing to be cared for and protected. In place of the empty hole in my heart, I gave too much of myself until I felt empty. I felt nothing would fill the void of not feeling loved. Over time I focused all of my energy into being the best me. My priority was to be the best athlete, the best daughter, the peacemaker, the idealist, the most creative, the best dress, the cleanest, the smartest, the funniest, the friendliest, and most lovable person I could be. The power to control people around me made me compulsive and left me vulnerable. My emotions were hard to hide so I became easy prey and an easy target.

ETERNAL BAGGAGE

I questioned God most days. I thought he was absent to protect me from evil. Endlessly I prayed everyday because everything scared me. Ironically I feared the things people did to me and most of all I was afraid to die and be alone. Was I alone? I was surrounded by tons of people, yet they were all the same. Malicious acts of unkindness haunted me. Embarking on the day to day challenges I experienced, I soon found myself alone distancing myself from others. As a result of secluding myself I could not grasp why everything seemed different. I hated negativity but felt completely lost without it. Was I obsessed with negativity? My demons were hard to live without even though they broke me down mentally.

Everyone and everything I encountered throughout my life left a smell, a taste, a memory, a sound, a feeling or insignificant trigger. I began trying to mend relationships with people that were unhealthy and distancing myself from those who had good intentions. Most of the time during occurrences it was hard for me to tell the difference. There were times when the tiniest red flag quickly shaped my opinion of someone. Separation was often difficult for me to endure. Even as an adult I would hold onto people who were not good for me. I am obsessed with trying to please others and put myself last in the process. I wanted to be around people all the time and did not realize there was always someone with me. Cliche as it sounds I was unaware that God never left me, he was carrying me when I was under the impression I was walking alone.

Today in this very moment I feel peace. I used all my experiences to help me grow into a better person. All these years I thought I was getting the short end of the stick, and I was merely gaining tools to help me be a better me. Over the years I learned it is normal to experience failure. I often reflected and thought about things too much! I analyzed I wasn't the failure, the people I encountered were failing me. I worked hard to eliminate the poisons in my life once I had children. I sacrificed so much for my children and loved them beyond the limits of motherhood to protect them. I created and molded two beautiful children into my expectations of what decent people should be.

Tranquility formed a bubble around me. I felt loved how I wanted to be loved all these years. No longer did I have to thirst for love from others. I accepted and received love from two people I created. Unconditionally I was respected and treated with such pure devotion from my two children. I had not known they were worthy of doing so and making me feel complete. There were no limits to the extent of expressing my love in return to my children. Cory and Mychelle were my main focus and every minute of my day was proof of how I adored them. I molded them into what my expectations of civilized people should be. That was my mission and it became a priority. It helped me to finally incorporate harmony in my chaotic life.

My goal is to be the perfect role model and model the behavior I expected in return. It wasn't easy! Everyday I fought to hide the hidden secrets of my life. Living in what I thought was peace often faded when my habits of being addicted to negativity poured over into being a mom. I'm only human so there were always times that I would backslide into old behaviors. Who could blame me? A person is always a product of their environment and in the end it eventually becomes part of their Eternal Baggage.